Annette Smith holds a place on my short shelf of social scientists with a deep and nuanced knowledge of A.A. Although I am always wary of what too easily turns into Procrustean efforts to fit a phenomenon such as Alcoholics Anonymous into larger schematic constructs, hers is one of the rare examples that avoids the traps and maximizes the value of such an approach.

> Ernest Kurtz, Ph.D., author of *Not-God: A History of Alcoholics Anonymous*

Alcoholics Anonymous has proliferated and is virtually omnipresent. It holds the greatest promise for recovery from alcoholism. But just what is A.A.? What does it consist of? Describing the structure of something that has no structure seems to be an impossible task, but Dr. Annette Smith has done just that. It is *a social world*, and the understanding of this concept clarifies A.A. and its success.

> Rabbi Dr. Abraham J. Twerski, Founder and Medical Director Emeritus of the Gateway Rehabilitation Center in Pittsburgh, and author of the best-selling *Addictive Thinking: Understanding Self-Deception*

With astute application of sociological concepts, Annette Smith unravels the processes by which Alcoholics Anonymous is successful in assisting alcohol-dependent men and women to become long-term sober citizens. Dr. Smith's careful qualitative research, based on personal interviews with A.A. members, captures the nuances of the self-transformation that occurs over time. Her investigation reveals that a combination of frequent meetings, the Twelve Steps, an encompassing concept of God and the pressure of groups and mentors that are integral to the A.A. program, have the unintended consequence of creating a *"larger whole than the sum of its parts."* A.A. members find themselves in a *social world* offering individuals of diverse personality types an ongoing sense of belonging that is as important to their general sense of well being as their continued sobriety. Parenthetically, Dr. Smith's analysis explains an aspect of A.A. that has puzzled many researchers in this field—why persons who have been sober for many years continue to attend A.A. meetings five, ten, fifteen or more years after their drinking problem is apparently cured.

> Jacqueline P. Wiseman, Ph.D., author of *Stations of the Lost: The Treatment of Skid Row Alcoholics*

Despite decades of analysis by scholars with different degrees of insider-ness, A.A. has limited systematic understanding by the communities of treatment and rehabilitation specialists. A diffuse sense of A.A.'s limitations is pervasive today, usually accompanied by groundless generalizations. Smith's study and its typological approach offers a large step forward in this pursuit, moving away from the misplaced question of "how's it work" to the question of "what are the many ways in which it works"? Her qualitative approach refines much quantitative data on A.A.'s limitations, recasting the questions into a framework of relative rather than absolute effects. This book can provide a magnificent introduction to A.A. for the serious student or for the counselor dedicated to an in-depth understanding of "how it works." At the same time, *Social World* offers a wealth of insights to established researchers and scholars. A great read!

> Paul M. Roman, Ph.D., Distinguished Research Professor and Director of the Center for Research on Behavioral Health and Human Service Delivery, University of Georgia

The Social World
of Alcoholics Anonymous

Hindsfoot Foundation Series on
Treatment and Recovery

Glenn F. Chesnut, Editor

The Social World of Alcoholics Anonymous

◆

How It Works

Annette R. Smith, Ph.D.

With an introduction by Linda Farris Kurtz, DPA

iUniverse, Inc.
New York Lincoln Shanghai

The Social World of Alcoholics Anonymous
How It Works

iUniverse books may be ordered through booksellers or by contacting:

iUniverse
2021 Pine Lake Road, Suite 100
Lincoln, NE 68512
www.iuniverse.com
1-800-Authors (1-800-288-4677)

Because of the dynamic nature of the Internet, any Web addresses
or links contained in this book may have changed
since publication and may no longer be valid.

ISBN: 978-0-595-47692-3 (pbk)
ISBN: 978-0-595-91956-7 (ebk)

Printed in the United States of America

To the memory of

Roger M.
April 11, 1937–January 2, 1991

Lee P.
November 7, 1927–December 1, 1990

Elaine B.
September 28, 1940–July 24, 2003

with love and gratitude

Contents

List of Tables and Figures

Preface

Although I am not myself a member of A.A., I have been intimately involved with the program and its membership for many years. In 1969, while I was working as a clinical social worker on the alcoholism treatment unit at a state mental hospital in California, the local A.A. Hospital and Institutions Committee asked to hold a meeting at the hospital. However, the administration said there were no rooms available. So, I arranged for the patients to be bussed to my house every Thursday night, where the meetings were held in my living room. This went on for almost a year until the hospital finally made a room available. During this initial exposure to A.A., I developed a close association with the fellowship, and through the years I have continued to attend open meetings and participate in many informal A.A. social activities.

In 1982, I returned to graduate school at the University of California, San Diego, to pursue my Ph.D. in sociology. As I developed my sociological interests, it seemed almost a natural progression in my involvement with A.A. to be able to look at it from the new perspective of scholarly research. The primary content of this book, including the data and references, was originally part of the dissertation submitted in 1991 in partial fulfillment of my Ph.D. in Sociology.

The theoretical and methodological approaches are those of symbolic interaction and qualitative field study. The focus is on interactive processes, which are not captured by survey research. Therefore, research efforts require the kind of intimate familiarity that can only be achieved through participant observation and other qualitative methods. The supportive data has been drawn primarily from participant observation over a twenty-three-year period in which I was associated with A.A. and from in-depth interviews with fifty-one members conducted in the course of the dissertation and previous research (Smith, 1986). Examples and citations presented included statements heard during several hundred open A.A. meetings in several geographic areas of the U.S. and abroad, and both professional and personal conversations with A.A. members. Additional material and interpretive insights have been drawn from the A.A. literature and referenced secondary sources. Interview subjects were initially recruited by placing notices on bulletin boards at four local A.A. social clubs and in chapter newsletters of the National Council on Alcoholism and the Employee Assistance Professionals Association. Interviews were limited to those with at least two years of continuous sobriety in an effort to provide some protection against harmful emotional effects to which those in early sobriety are vulnerable. As patterns of experiences began to emerge, additional subjects were sought through snowball sampling that focused on the need for stories reflecting these patterns.

The total interview sample consisted of twenty-eight men and twenty-three women, with ages ranging from nineteen to seventy. Length of sobriety ranged from two to over twenty years. All interviewees could be categorized as low middle to middle class, with occupations ranging from skilled labor to technical and professional. Three women and two men were unemployed at the time of the interview. Only one of the women categorized herself as a homemaker, and none of the subjects were retired. Ethnically, most were Caucasian, although one black male, one Native American male, and one Hispanic female were also in the sample. These variations did not appear to affect the general pattern of experiences reflected for those constructs under study.

A topic guide was used for interviews that established demographic information on age and other categories, including date of A.A. membership and date of current continuous sobriety. Questions addressed included the individual's perception of himself or herself in terms of interpersonal relationships and preferred ways of associating with others, how he or she first came to A.A., what happened there, feelings about what happened and ways in which the person has participated in A.A. since. The interviewees were also asked how and when they accepted themselves as alcoholic, and what they saw as most important in A.A. recovery. As the various chapters of this book were completed, they were read by selected

A.A. members for accuracy of organizational information and validity of suggested patterns and constructs. In the presentation of data, great care has been taken to protect the anonymity and confidentiality of all living A.A. members.

Subsequently, a new edition of the Big Book of Alcoholics Anonymous was issued (AAWS, 2001), and several noteworthy works have been added to the qualitative research literature. A paper on the social construction of group dependency based on a chapter of the dissertation was published (Smith, 1993). Makela, Arminen, Bloomfield, *et al.* (1996) compared the development of A.A. as a social movement in eight societies; Wilcox (1998), Jensen (1999) and Pollner and Stein (2001) provided studies of aspects of A.A. culture; and O'Halloran (2003) examined differences between ethnographic and ethnomethodological (conversation analysis) methods in studying Alcoholics Anonymous. Other relevant publications on the subject include L. Kurtz's (1997) handbook for practitioners on self-help and support groups, which references some of the material included in the dissertation, and Bishop and Pittman's (1994) second volume of their A.A. bibliography.

While I am a friend and supporter of A.A., I recognize that it may not be the way to recovery for all alcoholics, and certainly is not the only way, as A.A. itself recognizes (AAWS, 1976:xx). But this work is not intended as either a paean or critique. It is intended to establish the social world perspective for studying A.A., and highlights the interactive processes in A.A. success and the re-socialization that brings it about.

Acknowledgments

As this book is based on research conducted for my doctoral dissertation, I would like to acknowledge the help of my original doctoral committee at the University of California, San Diego: Drs. Jacqueline Wiseman, Rae Blumberg, Lowell Storms and Lola Ross, and the late Drs. Fred Davis and Mary Pendery. Others who assisted me by providing materials and supportive comments for that research were the late Dr. Harrison Trice of Cornell University, Dr. Ernest Kurtz of the University of Michigan, the staff at UCSD Extension Alcohol, Tobacco and Other Drug Studies, Susan U. of the General Service staff of Alcoholics Anonymous and Paul C. of the Alcoholics Anonymous Archives Committee. Drs. Paul Roman and Terry Blum provided much encouragement whenever we met at conferences, and Dr. Anita Harbert at the SDSU School of Social Work provided me with backup for my duties there so that I could take time to complete my writing.

I am especially grateful to all members of the fellowship of Alcoholics Anonymous who shared their lives with me at meetings, in social situations and in research interviews. Sharon B., Claudette O., the late Lee P., Ernie H., and the late Elaine B. were some of those A.A. members who read chapters of my dissertation and helped to validate depictions of the A.A. social world and the conclusions drawn.

In helping me to prepare my dissertation for this book, I very much appreciate the critical review and invaluable input of Dianne Chalfant, Drs. Ernest and Linda Farris Kurtz, Dr. Paul Roman of the University of Georgia, Rabbi Dr. Abraham J. Twerski of the Gateway Rehabilitation Center in Pennsylvania, Dr. Glenn F. Chesnut of Indiana University (and the Hindsfoot Foundation), and once more, Dr. Jacqueline Wiseman, my primary mentor in my sociological studies. Thanks to Charlie Bishop, Jr., for introducing my original dissertation to Ernie Kurtz, initiating his interest in my work, and to Elizabeth Knefel of the UCSD library for her help in tracking down lost reference information.

Finally, thanks to my children, Margie Glickman Jones, Rainee Glickman and Andy Glickman, and my companion of the past eight years, Tony Balyeat, for their moral support during the completion of this book.

Introduction

by Linda Farris Kurtz, DPA

Professor Emeritus, Eastern Michigan University School of Social Work, author of *Self-Help and Support Groups: A Handbook for Practitioners*

I first became acquainted with Annette Smith's approach to the sociological study of A.A. a number of years ago, via her doctoral dissertation. One of the best examples of qualitative research on A.A. which I had come across, the social world framework which she provided offered a practical and down-to-earth analysis. It is one I have turned to and cited often in my research, writing and teaching career since that time. In this present book, Smith further clarifies the social world concept while also illuminating our understanding of the fellowship. Her exacting description of A.A. will introduce the organization to those who know nothing about it and enlighten those who know something, but not everything.

Smith's application of a conversion typology further shows the complexity and variation of recovering styles and how conversion to a new identity comes though numerous processes of conversion and not simply through brainwashing or coercion, as is often thought.

You hear it said that A.A. is not for everyone, but many who initially reject it urgently need it. As helpers and bystanders we must understand that the process of inclusion in A.A. is not uniform. There are different paths to affiliation and that is what Annette Smith makes clear in her study of A.A. participation. This is important for anyone who works in the alcoholism field or does research on recovery.

At the heart of her careful analysis is the idea that group dependency can be "constructed" by and for those who are not natural joiners in order for them to become integrated within the A.A. support system. Clarifying how some newcomers may not fit in or take to the group, but later become attached to it, contributes greatly to understanding the process of affiliation. Otherwise, we assume that the dropout is a person for whom A.A. holds no hope. Classifying this kind of person as an "individualist" shows that he or she can make as much use of A.A. as those who are more group-oriented if properly assisted while in recovery. As part of this clarification, Smith highlights the importance of dyadic relationships in early recovery. This is significant for professional counselors (social workers) who can introduce newcomers to someone who takes on the role of temporary sponsor.

1

Foundations for a Sociological Study of A.A.

A.A. as a Subject for Study

Since it was founded in 1935, Alcoholics Anonymous has become fertile ground for research in alcoholism rehabilitation and recovery. A.A. is perceived as a quasi-religious program leading to behavioral change through attitude adjustment and mutual support. Its philosophy, precepts and tools of change are a syncretic blending of scientific and religious values and practices which are taught through written and oral language and by example, within a context of group interaction which creates a process of adult re-socialization. The program, its history and philosophy, its value as treatment, its bases of affiliation and the experiences of its members have been widely examined (e.g. Bean, 1975; Blumberg, 1977; Thune, 1977; Kurtz, 1979; Trice, 1957, 1958; Trice and Roman, 1970a, 1970b; Maxwell, 1984; Brown, 1985; Rudy, 1986; Denzin, 1987). It has been studied as a social movement (Conrad and Schneider, 1980; Room, 1993; Makela, *et al.*, 1996) and as part of the history of addiction treatment and rehabilitation (Vaillant, 1984; White, 1998). Recently, researchers have begun to study cultural aspects of A.A. more thoroughly (Wilcox, 1998; Jensen, 1999). Personal accounts are so numerous as to make an exhaustive list almost impossible. One source for such publications can be found however in the two lengthy bibliographies assembled by Bishop and Pittman: *The Annotated Bibliography of Alcoholics Anonymous, 1939–1989* and *To Be Continued—The Alcoholics Anonymous World Bibliography, 1935–1994* (Bishop and Pittman, 1989; 1994).[1]

Theories about key factors leading to A.A. success have included A.A.'s open door accessibility (Bales, 1945), change from internal to external locus of control (Bridgman, 1987), redefining the negative labeling (Trice, 1970, Grove, 1984), the intense group support (Mechanic, 1978) and certain psychosocial factors and psychological characteristics of those who affiliate with A.A. (Button, 1956; Trice, 1957; Trice and Roman, 1970b).

Above all, there is an overriding consensus that central to individual success in A.A. is the achievement, through following the guidelines of the program, of individual "conversions" or transformations of identity which lead to the adoption of new values, new ways of relating and a new way of living (Kurtz, 1979; Thune, 1977; Rooney, 1985; Denzin, 1987).

Kurtz (1979) describes the paradoxes of the A.A. precepts, the most primary of which is that freedom depends on surrender. That is, one must give up control in order to have it. This begins when the alcoholic accepts that above all, he or she is "not God." Thune (1977) and Jensen (1999) stress the importance of the telling of life stories in helping members connect their lives and see evidence that the practice of the principles indeed "work." Thune (1977) also clarifies the point that success depends on a phenomenological acceptance of the alcoholic self-identity—i.e. alcoholism is not only something one has, but at a deeper existential level, is at the heart of one's being. The Big Book of Alcoholics Anonymous (AAWS, 1976; 2001) approaches conversion from the standpoint of a spiritual experience, whereas others approach it in a more social psychological language as a transformation of self (Rooney, 1985) or identity (Denzin, 1987). Nevertheless, it represents the same radical transformation of self as found in the definition of conversion (Travisano, 1970:594, in Lofland and Skonovd, 1982:375).

Studying A.A. as a Social World

The term social organization refers to the structure of social relations within a group, usually relations between subgroups and institutions.

Sociologists have identified several forms of social organization. In his 1983 book, *Invisible Lives: Social Worlds of the Aged*, David Unruh described features of the following six forms of social organization:

(1) A *formal organization*, such as a corporation, with a hierarchy of official roles and a strong bureaucratic authority structure.

(2) A *territorial community*, such as a town with a weak authority structure, informal roles, and membership based on spatial closeness.

(3) An *interest group*, such as an environmental advocacy group, with a moderate authority structure, and shared interest in a particular issue as its basis for involvement.

(4) A *voluntary association*, such as the Parent Teacher Association at a local school, with formal membership rolls, a hierarchy of officers, moderate influence of authority, and fairly formal roles.

(5) An *informal group*, such as a book club, with a lack of stable structure, informal roles, and shared interest in a particular topic or activity as its basis for involvement.

(6) Lastly, a *social world*, such as the world of tennis or that of the aged, with a broad, loosely structured, interconnected environment, potentially large population, and common interest as its basis of involvement.

A social world has a structure which is highly permeable, which means that membership is voluntary, and people move in and out of it with ease. There is an absence of a formal hierarchy, and the influence of leadership is weak. Social roles are highly informal. Nevertheless, it is a fairly defined entity with a technology and language of its own that is passed on to its members through various means of communication.

As an organization, A.A. has previously been considered to be a voluntary association, and studies of it as such have focused on its formal structure and activities (Gellman, 1964). However, there are several characteristics of voluntary associations, such as formal membership rolls and a hierarchy of officers, that do not match with A.A.'s social organization. On the other hand, A.A. has also been referred to as a social world (Shibutani, 1961) or part of a larger social world of recovery (Denzin 1987). This would be in keeping with several organizational aspects of A.A., starting with the fact that its formal organization is loosely structured, without a hierarchy of authority. At the basic level, meetings are conducted by leaders who are elected by the group to serve on a rotating basis. Local A.A. groups are formed into Districts, which are in turn included in what is called an Area. Each Area in the U.S. and Canada elects a Delegate who attends an annual A.A. General Service Conference in New York City, where they vote on matters affecting A.A. as a whole.

While the formal organization of A.A. is part of what makes it fit the definition of a social world, it is much larger than just this formal organization. It is an extended "universe of mutual response" (Shibutani, 1961), made up of a network of loosely connected organizations and relationships, involving both formal and informal components and activities. These include recovery homes which provide room and board for newcomers, and A.A. clubhouses (Alano clubs) which provide a variety of social activity for members and their families. These entities may sponsor picnics, dances, ball games, and other activities which are set up completely outside the formal organizational structure of A.A. There are also strictly informal interactions which have rarely been studied. Members going out for coffee after an A.A. meeting, getting together for a New Year's Eve party, or clusters of old timers meeting for breakfast and being sought out for advice by other members are just a few examples of informal aspects of the A.A. social world.

The Advantages of
the Social World Approach

Some studies have provided considerable insight into member experiences (Maxwell, 1984) and some frameworks for viewing these experiences (Leach and Norris, 1977; Rudy, 1986; Denzin, 1987). Maxwell's work (1984) presented first person accounts that illustrated the dynamics of the

A.A. meeting and the feelings of members about their experience and what it meant to their recovery. He suggested that meeting attendance alone did not bring success, and that one must become "immersed" in the "fellowship." But the process of this immersion is not clearly described. Leach and Norris (1977) developed a framework for viewing the process of A.A. affiliation in phases which lead to abstinence, and Rudy (1986) presented a model of stages which attempted to address the affiliative process as one that went beyond the achievement of abstinence, and focused on the shaping of affiliation. Both models designated each stage as a specific act or event.[2]

Rudy also established a typology of A.A. careers based on the sequence of A.A. participation and acceptance of the alcoholic self-identity and on the emphasis placed on drinking experiences in testimonials. However, Rudy did not elaborate on the connection between the processes of interaction in the A.A. social world and the development of his Convinced and Converted types from the standpoint of their own experiences.[3]

In this book, I will assert that by studying A.A. from a social world perspective, and evaluating the informal social environment as well as the formal meeting environment, it is possible to see that social integration into the social world of A.A. is a key to success, and to show the process by which this integration occurs, as well as variations in the pathways to that integration and in the experiences of conversion. I will present data to demonstrate that in A.A. the progressive involvement in the larger social network fosters the interactive processes that lead to successful recovery.

I will offer a typology of A.A. members that represents types of social world participants, rather than of alcoholics, and show why this is a more useful approach. Furthermore, the dimensions that inform this typology focus on content of conversion experience rather than sequence, and on social world integration, rather than on any specific aspect of one's basis of affiliation (i.e., emphasis on drinking problems).

The Organization of this Book

The next chapter, Chapter 2, will describe the applicability to A.A. of those organizational features that distinguish social world from other forms of social organization. Relying on the definition of a social world provided by Shibutani (1961), developed by Strauss (1978), and further refined by Unruh (1979, 1980), I will describe A.A. as a social world. Utilizing a framework developed by Unruh (1979) I will illustrate types of social world participation in A.A. and the process of social integration, including aspects of A.A. social life and involvement of A.A. members in intersecting social worlds. It will be shown that successful A.A. membership depends on integration into the social world to the level of Regulars who are committed to its continuance, and Insiders who create the social world for others.

In Chapter 3, I will focus on the notion of affiliative needs and group dependency among members, as these are described by Trice and Roman (1970b), as associated with successful A.A. affiliation, and demonstrate how, through the social construction of reality (Berger and Luckman, 1966), some people who do not reflect these characteristics nevertheless may become integrated into the A.A. social world.

Chapter 4 will examine the experiences of A.A. members in achieving transformation of self, called the A.A. conversion. These experiences will be described within a framework of religious conversion motifs developed by Lofland and Skonovd (1980) as they apply at different stages of the A.A. conversion career. I will use a model of four stages of that career that are expressed in terms of functional time periods in the process rather than of specific events.

Finally in Chapter 5, I will offer my own typology consisting of two broad types of A.A. participant. Specifically, these types will be described in terms of a high or low level of group dependency and affiliative need, group versus individual focus in social world participation, and primarily cognitive versus primarily affective or emotional content of conversion experience.

2

The Social World of A.A.

From the work of Strauss (1978) and others we have learned to conceptualize social worlds in broad terms, such as the social world of tennis, of music, etc. However, it would seem that the social world perspective might also apply if a particular organizational structure is such that its name implies a larger frame of reference than its formal structure and it meets other criteria of the social world definition. In the case of A.A., the egalitarian, non-hierarchical nature of its structure, its lack of specific spatial or physical boundaries, and its fairly rapid worldwide growth and spawning of other related programs and activities, seem to have taken it beyond the limited size and scope of the traditional voluntary association.

Analytical Framework

The Social World Perspective

Shibutani (1978) first defined a social world as "a universe of mutual response ... a cultural arena whose boundaries are set neither by territory nor formal membership, but by the limits of effective communication" (Shibutani, 1978:119). Strauss (1978) saw the social world perspective as one from which it is possible to discover the processes of social change by which new shared definitions and symbolic meanings come about, and he elaborated on a number of features of social worlds. Among the most critical of these are: that people enter a social world based on a perception of a common bond, and that membership is voluntary and fluid. There are no formal membership rolls, dues or organizational hierarchies. There are

shared values and perspectives, and a common unique language that iden-
tifies and supports identification. Activities may be both formal and informal, and social interactions between and among members tend to be
unlimited by the parameters of the common bond. Furthermore, as a
social world develops and expands, it may cross with or give rise to others,
so that they are part of a network of intersecting social worlds.

Unruh (1983) further refined the social world definition to encompass
a broader context that may include the other forms of social organization
as part of the social world. For example, in his studies of the aging, the
social world includes those voluntary associations, formal associations and
interest groups that address the interests and concerns of the senior population.

Levels of Social World Involvement

Another typology developed by Unruh (1980) pertains to levels of involvement in a social world. These are defined by the scope of that involvement
and the degree to which participants are absorbed in that particular social
world as opposed to others. Involvement is the key to social integration
into a particular social world.

Unruh's typology of individual involvement consists of Strangers,
Tourists, Regulars and Insiders. Each type is characterized along four
dimensions:

1) Orientation to the social world

2) How it is experienced

3) The nature of the relationships within it

4) Commitment to its values, activities and continuance

Strangers are naïve in their orientation, not able to distinguish this
social world from others in which they participate. Their experience
within it is one of disorientation in that they do not know the rules. Their

relationships are superficial and they feel little if any commitment. Strangers are those who are outside the social world and who may or may not be potential members. Some may be excluded from membership by virtue of the fact that they do not share the common element that creates the basic condition for the existence of the particular universe of discourse. But others who are potential members must become members through "voluntary identification" (Unruh, 1980:161).

Tourists have an orientation of curiosity toward the social world. Their experience is limited to certain relevant concerns such as participation as a means to acquire social status. Relationships within the social world are based on some kind of reward, and there is, again, little if any commitment. Tourists are those who are "involved only to the extent that their participation remains entertaining, profitable or diversionary" (Unruh, 1980:163). The difference between Strangers and Tourists is that Tourists "have found a certain degree of relevance in a social world and have continued involvement" in it (Unruh, 1980:163).

Regulars are characterized by an orientation of habituation, an experience of integration, with relationships of familiarity, and a commitment to ongoing functioning of the social world. They are reliable in their attendance or attention to social world activities. Regulars are the backbone and the core of the social world. They are distinguished from Tourists in that they have established identification with the social world and a "commitment, which sustains them through good times and bad" (Unruh, 1980:164).

Finally, Insiders have an orientation which functions to bring about a total identity. Their experience is one that helps to create the social world for others. Their relationships are characterized by intimacy and they are committed to action and engagement in recruiting others. They have an intimate knowledge of the procedures and the technology of the social world. The involvement of Insiders "may very well encompass the entire life-round of the person" (Unruh, 1980:164).

A recapitulation of this typology is illustrated in Table 1.

Table 1

Levels of Social World Involvement

	Strangers	Tourists	Regulars	Insiders
Orientation	Naivete	Curiosity	Habituation	Total Identity
Experience	Disorientation	Relevancy to Concerns	Integration	Creativity
Relationships	Superficiality	Reward-basis	Familiarity	Intimacy
Commitment	Little if any	Little if any	Reliability	Recruitment

It is suggested that members in a particular social world may exemplify each of these types at different times or stages of their membership careers, and that there may be a relationship between their level of participation and degree of satisfaction or benefit derived from their association with that social world.

This typology will be used as a framework for examining A.A. participation as it may vary among members and during the course of an A.A. career. It will be shown that changes in these types of participation, even where commitment to the basic values and goals of A.A. remains, tend to occur as they relate to changes in the following four criteria:

1) Perceived need for the structured activities of the social world

2) Perceived need for supportive interaction with others in the social world

3) Priority of close personal relationships in A.A. versus those in competing social worlds

4) Priority of activities in A.A. versus those in competing social worlds

The data will also suggest that, depending on the already achieved level of integration, the bases of the circumstantial changes and the nature of the competing worlds, the resultant changes in A.A. involvement may sometimes play an important role in successful recovery.

A.A. as a Social World

The following sections will describe those features that define A.A. as a social world in accord with Unruh's (1983) framework, and provide some discussion of two aspects of that social world that have previously received little attention in the literature. These aspects are:

1) Informal activities and relationships in the social world of A.A., and

2) Developing intersecting social worlds

Defining the Social World

The most succinct definition of A.A. as a social world is contained in the opening of its meeting preamble:

> Alcoholics Anonymous is a fellowship of men and women who share their experience, strength and hope with each other that they may solve their common problem.... Our primary purpose is to stay sober and help other alcoholics to achieve sobriety. (*A.A. Grapevine*, 1947)

The concept of "fellowship" suggests a non-hierarchical approach to association, and the notion of "sharing" establishes that A.A. is a universe of discourse or mutual response.[4] The focus on the common problem of achieving and maintaining sobriety suggests the basis for the cognitive identification as well as shared interests and concerns.

Despite the fact that A.A.'s Traditions specify that "an A.A. group ought never endorse, finance or lend the A.A. name to any related facility or outside enterprise" (A.A., 1976:564), which means that A.A. itself does not operate or ally itself with other activities, a social world has grown up around it which includes far more than the original recovery groups or their corporate entity. For purposes of this discussion, the social world of A.A. will encompass both the official organization of Alcoholics Anonymous and those formal and informal associations that are specifically related, but not those that are only related through borrowing of A.A. technology or because of a similar interest in alcoholism recovery.

Thus the elements which will be considered part of the social world of A.A. include the basic meeting groups, special purpose groups (e.g., young people's, teachers, doctors, lawyers, and nurses groups), connecting inter-groups, area assemblies, national and international conferences, the General Service Board of Alcoholics Anonymous, Inc. and its two subsidiary corporations, World Services (which publishes A.A. literature) and *The A.A. Grapevine* (the A.A. periodical), and their national and district offices or service centers. It includes A.A.-sponsored social events, such as dances, picnics and dinners. Although not part of official A.A., the social world will also include alcoholism rehabilitation houses or recovery homes, which are generally operated by and for A.A. members, and Alano clubs, which are private social clubs for A.A. members and their families or associates.

It will not include separate family programs, similar programs designed to address addictions other than alcoholism, or professional treatment programs. These will be considered part of a larger social world of recovery, and will be discussed in the section on intersecting social worlds.[5]

The A.A. Sphere of Influence—Population Encompassed. Compared to other forms of social organization, the potential population of a social world is almost unlimited. Rather than being dependent on such features as physical location, membership rosters, and visibility of others, it is limited only by the common bond which draws attention to it and the extent to which "information and knowledge about its existence is available or restricted" (Unruh, 1983:31). Thus, membership in the social world is not dependent on any formal admission procedure, but on the direction of that attention upon it and the "derivation of personal identity" from it (Unruh, 1983:31).

The history of A.A. as an organization began in 1935 with its two cofounders in Akron, Ohio. In 1986, membership was estimated at over one million, with more than 85,000 groups worldwide, and is now reported to be over two million (AAWS, 2004).[6] Since its foundation is personal anonymity, there are no formal membership rolls.[7] Activities take place in a variety of community settings such as churches, schools, hospitals, alcoholism treatment centers, rehabilitation houses, Alano clubs, and even private homes. To the extent that the ecology of the meeting places allow, A.A. symbols such as its logo and wall plaques containing the Twelve Steps are displayed. Tables with literature may be set up. However, there is no fixed location on which A.A. is dependent for its existence.

It is, of course, unlikely that persons who do not have a drinking problem would involve themselves in A.A. Although accurate numbers are difficult to obtain because of variations in sampling and collection methodologies, some estimates of the number of adults in the U.S. alone with alcohol problems are as high as 18 million, with half or more having symptoms of alcoholism.[8] Therefore, the potential membership of A.A. worldwide would seem to be quite large. Furthermore, as suggested, the social world which has grown up around it often includes family members and significant others in the alcoholic's life, so that the upper boundaries of potential identification with the total social world of recovery may be even larger.

As in all social worlds, membership is based only on the direction of attention placed upon it and on the personal identity members derive from affiliation. As one long-time member explained:

> It was not until I got here that I really knew where I fit in … and I found out it was O.K. to be an alcoholic as long as I didn't drink a day at a time, and let this program work in my life.

Defining A.A. Membership—The Dominant Boundary Characteristic. As opposed to other forms of social organization, the essential determinant of social world boundaries is the "cognitive identification of the people involved," rather than any formal recognition of membership. "If individuals perceive themselves as integrated, and are viewed by others as such, or engage in activities that link them into the concerns of a social world, then they are at least marginally integrated" (Unruh, 1983:33). The only official requirement for A.A. membership is a "desire to stop drinking" (AAWS, 1976:564). It is significant that A.A. makes no diagnosis of alcoholism, has no specific enrollment protocol and does not give formal recognition to membership. As one member put it, "If you believe you are a member of A.A., you are!"

Indeed, although those who affiliate with it are referred to as members, the term is misleading, since membership is solely constituted by this cognitive identification. Despite the fact that many do not come to their first A.A. meetings voluntarily, but are sent, even required, to come by judges, health practitioners, employers or family members, continuing long term membership in A.A. is voluntary.[9] In order to develop the cognitive identification necessary, the newcomer must become integrated into the social world through the process of engaging in its activities. In this way, he or she may come to view him or herself, and be viewed by others, as at least marginally integrated. Sometimes this happens almost immediately. An A.A. woman friend in her seventies with twenty years of sobriety explained: "I knew I belonged the first time I went to a meeting. I felt the people there knew how to get what I wanted."

But for other people, this cognitive identification may take time to develop, as reflected in a commonly heard statement to newcomers: "Get the body to the meeting, and the mind will follow."

Thus, one does not "join" A.A. in the formal sense. One becomes a member by voluntary association with the ideals and practices. Furthermore, membership is fluid and constantly changing both in composition and degrees of participation. One's leaving or ending participation often receives the response from others of a shrug and a reflective comment, such as: "He still has more drinking to do!"

Although meetings are held in specific locations, membership is not bound to location or time, but is expressed in the communication and practice of the A.A. technology which consists of the Twelve Steps to personal recovery, the Twelve Traditions governing the fellowship and the slogans to help with daily living (e.g., Easy Does It, One Day at a Time, First Things First, etc.).

Getting In and Out—Permeability of Organization Structure. While some forms of social organization may restrict entry into their domain by setting requirements of eligibility and processes of acceptance, people move in and out of social worlds easily and without the need for formal recognition. Unruh asserts that this fluidity may "complicate the matter of determining the values, roles and evaluation of those within" due to a continual entry of new ideas and practices (Unruh, 1983:34).

Despite A.A.'s focus on alcoholism, becoming part of the social world is not determined by labels imposed by outside sources or by A.A. itself. Although accepting one's alcoholism is considered critical for recovery, the identification of that alcoholism must be made by the individual member through the association of his or her situation with those described in the literature and with the life stories shared and heard at meetings and in other interactions in the A.A. social world. Furthermore, membership in A.A. is not restricted by any formal rules of inclusion or exclusion,[10] and is highly permeable. As one young man put it: "All I had to do was show up."

Informal Obstacles. Some researchers and other observers have noted that A.A. has traditionally been, and continues to be, essentially a "male club" (e.g., Sandmaier, 1980), and that its principles, values and language have tended to informally exclude those from population groups not comfortable with its decidedly middle class belief system (e.g., alcoholism as sickness rather than moral weakness) or practices (e.g., the open sharing of personal problems).[11] But then, studies have tended to discount the impact of social class on A.A. affiliation and participation (Murphy, 1952; Lofland, 1960), and to suggest that psychological issues are more important than sociological ones (Trice and Roman, 1970a). Furthermore, the number of women in A.A. has increased over the years, and they have begun to infiltrate even the higher levels of A.A. leadership. Women For Sobriety, an alternative program for women started in the mid-1970s, generally failed to draw large numbers of alcoholic women, who seemed to prefer affiliating with A.A. However, many of the women in A.A. credit their successful affiliation to the support found in women-only meetings. As one woman in her forties expressed it in a casual conversation: "I love this program, and there are no bad meetings. But it was the women's meetings that really saved my ass!"

The issue of ethnic minority representation in A.A. is somewhat more complex, and data has not always been available from A.A. surveys. However, according to the most recent survey, minority groups reportedly comprise about 10% of the membership, including Blacks, Hispanics, Native Americans and Asians (AAWS, 2004). It is likely that programs in urban areas over the past several decades fostered this increase in minority group membership. For example, in southern California, with its proximity to the Mexican border, A.A. meeting schedules show a number of Spanish-speaking meetings, which suggests an increase of Hispanic membership. On the other hand, meetings and other activities in the social world still tend to be naturally segregated by geography, i.e., "ghettoized," and it is still fairly unusual to see much of an ethnic mix at "uptown" meetings. As one interviewee, a black man in his late forties, told me:

> It's not that hard for me, having been in the service and school and all, but most of us just don't feel comfortable at those meetings … not that we are made unwelcome or anything … just that usually we're the only one of us there.

There are, of course, other social factors that also may mitigate against membership, not the least of which are those physical discomforts sometimes present. As one member expressed it:

> With the endless chatter about drunkalogs [stories about drinking], the smoke in the rooms, the coffee drinking, the same old jokes over and over again, one has to be a special individual indeed to stay around A.A.!

Nevertheless, the growth of A.A. attests to the fact that many people are not deterred by these factors, or they are able to form meetings with special rules that eliminate some of the features they find distasteful. A recent trend, for example, is the dramatic increase in the number of nonsmoking meetings.

Traditions and Rules—Influence of Authority Structure. Although all forms of social organizations develop some authority structures to formulate policy, disseminate information, make decisions regarding procedures, etc., social worlds have limited or no central authority. Since a social world may encompass and include other forms of social organization, there may be multiple authority structures present. This might imply "pockets of rigidity within an otherwise loose and amorphous system" (Unruh, 1983:34). Another possibility is that direct influence is primarily located in various "subworlds" of the social world (Unruh, 1983). Such subworlds may be based on geographic location or other bases of segmentation.

As an organization, A.A. is loosely structured. Rather than specific rules of order, it is governed by a set of principles for group membership and participation (the Twelve Traditions). These contain guidelines for the conduct of members and groups, including financial support, involvement in outside interests, public relations and maintaining anonymity (AAWS, 1976:564).[12]

The primary organizational unit is the group, which may vary in size, and of which there are apt to be many in any sizable community. A group is defined as a spiritual entity having but one primary purpose, that of carrying its message to the alcoholic who "still suffers" (AAWS, 1976:565). Some groups meet once a week, but other groups may hold several meetings each week. Members attend as many meetings of as many groups as they choose, and anywhere they choose, although they may designate one particular group as their "home group." Each group is "autonomous except in matters affecting other groups or A.A. as a whole" (AAWS, 1976:564).

The governance of A.A. is provided through a service structure that includes elected representatives from each group who are called General Service Representatives (GSRs), and meet monthly as part of a District

Committee. This Committee carries out A.A. work, which may include the distribution of literature, the publishing of meeting schedules, working with the community, and operating the local A.A. service centers. The District Committee also elects a representative, or District Committee Member (DCM), who attends quarterly Area Assemblies. An Area may represent a whole state or a part of a state. The purpose of Area Assemblies is to discuss issues of concern to A.A. in that particular Area.

Every two years, the Area Assembly elects a Delegate to represent it at the annual General Service Conference in New York, the purpose of which is to resolve matters of concern to A.A., to approve new literature, and to recommend actions to the fellowship as a whole. These recommendations or suggestions are rolled down the line to the individual groups.

In some cities, an additional layer is added in the form of an Intergroup Association which coordinates A.A. work in that city and the surrounding urban area. These Intergroups, while not an official part of the A.A. service structure, are nevertheless recognized as a more convenient and efficient way of conducting A.A. business in high population municipalities.

The General Service Board of twenty-one members (fourteen A.A. members and seven non-alcoholics) operates the two subsidiary corporations (Alcoholics Anonymous World Services, Inc. and The Grapevine, Inc.), and has overall responsibility for the General Service Office, which coordinates A.A. worldwide service efforts. At each level, there are various committees that carry out the work of the Intergroup, District, Area or Board. These include committees for business operations, program, hospital and institutions work, and cooperation with the professional community, to name a few.

According to the A.A. Traditions, leaders are to be "but trusted servants; they do not govern" (AAWS,1976:564). Meetings are conducted by a leader who is responsible for following the meeting format. There is also a secretary who is responsible for conducting group business such as collecting donations to pay for room rent, coffee, and literature. The leader and secretary are selected by the group, usually to serve on a rotating basis. Other officers who may be called on to report at a meeting include a treasurer, a General Service Representative and an Intergroup Representative.

Terms of office may be as short as one or two weeks, or as long as two years. For example, while leaders may change with every meeting or so, a secretary is usually elected for at least a six month term to provide some stability to the business end of the group's functioning.

However, since there is no central authority overseeing these practices, there are exceptions, and some meetings may be conducted in more authoritarian fashion than others. For example, one meeting in the local community where I did my research was known to have had a single person running the meeting, not for months, but for several years. A friend who has been in A.A. for many years calls this meeting his home group. He told me: "Jack considers this his meeting, and it's a solid meeting. So why try to change it?"

Again, due to this lack of strong central authority, direct influence on everyday activities and practices are sometimes located in various "sub-worlds." These may be based on geography (e.g., southern California A.A., East Coast A.A.), or other common characteristics (e.g. young people in A.A., gay and lesbian recovery groups, Spanish-speaking groups). One may hear actual reference to these differences in the process of the meeting. For example, when introducing the celebration of a milestone in sobriety, the leader of one meeting remarked: "In southern California it is customary to recognize ninety days of continued abstinence by the giving of a token."

The pockets of rigidity referred to by Unruh may also be found, but largely in the more formal organizations which make up the social world. For instance, while one is not automatically ejected from a meeting for coming to it obviously under the influence of alcohol, residents of a rehab house must adhere to strict rules of alcohol abstinence, and a violator could be made to leave. A young man in his twenties whom I met in the Alano Club lounge explained:

> I had thirty days [abstinence] at [ABC] House, but I blew it Saturday night and they kicked me out. Now I have two, and I want to get back in.

There are also certain meeting groups that are known for having more rigid approaches than others about who may be allowed admittance to the meeting. For example, a closed men's meeting attended primarily by a group of "old timers" and those they sponsor, makes it a point to let people know informally that, although officially anyone with a drinking problem is welcome at A.A., "druggies" are not welcome at their meetings. As one man from this group told me:

> As long as they come as an alcoholic, it's fine. But the ones that go on and on about their drug problems ... well that's not what A.A. is about.

Norms and Sanctions. Gellman described A.A. norms as informal and having "evolved out of the historical origins of the association" (1964:108). They are essentially guided by the program technology, especially the Twelve Traditions, but some are unwritten. Many contrast with norms in the society at large in the degree of strictness or permissiveness. For example, while sobriety is a norm in the dominant culture, it is not defined as complete abstinence from alcohol as it is in the fellowship.

On the other hand, in other areas such as following organizational protocol and observing status structures, A.A. norms may be markedly less strict. As previously stated, relationships and roles are basically egalitarian, and everyone is known by first name without respect to titles bestowed or degrees earned. Since A.A. membership occurs simultaneously with membership in other social worlds, this may require that A.A. members develop a means of shifting from this egalitarian base to more hierarchical ones in the dominant social structure (Westermann, 1978).

Protocol in A.A. is relaxed. Although meetings are structured, attendance is not regulated, and people come and go throughout a meeting without sanction. Another area where norms are relaxed is in the area of language permitted at meetings. While not admired or encouraged, the use of off-color language, even four-letter words, is not uncommon. While many may not like it or even be offended by it, it is accepted as a legitimate form of expression for some people. As one older woman explained:

I guess I'm used to it a little now. But at first, it kind of shocked me. I still don't like it, and I try to stay away from the meetings where I know there will be a lot.

In some cases, it may be considered a part of a person's problem, and that is, after all, what they are there for in the first place. As one long-time member said of a young newcomer whose language was rather offensive: "Give him time. If he sticks around and works the program, you'll see that stuff start to go."

The primary feature of normative functioning in A.A. appears to be not the norms themselves, but how violations are handled. For instance, although it is a violation of normative behavior in A.A. to come to a meeting smelling of alcohol or obviously intoxicated, the violator is not ejected from the meeting unless he or she is disruptive. Even in that case, he or she may be led by one or two others to another room and instead of being given a reprimand, talked to with understanding and empathy. However if the person is not disruptive, he or she may simply be allowed to remain at the meeting. In fact, it is sometimes said of such a person: "He's in the right place!"

Indeed, sanctions and responses to violations of behavioral norms in A.A. are not formalized, but are left to the "group conscience." Thus, it can be decided by group vote how to handle any problem which presents itself. Among the highest order of normative behaviors is the protection of one's own and other members' anonymity. According to the A.A. Traditions (AAWS, 1976:564):

> 11. We need always maintain personal anonymity at the level of press, radio and films.

> 12. Anonymity is the spiritual foundation of all our Traditions, ever reminding us to place principles before personalities.

Thus, in A.A. surnames are most often not used at all, and people are referred to by given name and last initial (e.g., Susie B., Roger M.) or by nicknames based on occupation, place of birth, hobby or other identifying feature (e.g., Boston Charlie, Doctor Bob, Motorcycle Pete). Sometimes nicknames are associated with anecdotes from a member's life story. For example, a woman who left her Christmas tree decorations up for three years waiting for her soldier son's return during wartime, was given the descriptive "Christmas tree" preceding her first name. Members who introduce each other in the earshot of the public do so by using a coded introduction, the meaning of which only social world participants would be likely to understand, and which will not be revealed here.[13]

New Addicts and the Rate of Organization Change. In social worlds, the absence of a strong central authority structure and lack of spatial limits or rigid bureaucracy, are conducive to rapid social change. Changes tend to be more spontaneous than in other forms of social organization that are bound by requirements such as formal member approval (Unruh, 1983).

In A.A., these effects have been especially prominent. Although the basic ideology and integrity of purpose of the fellowship have been held relatively intact through the years, with changes in the technology made only as a result of formal policy decisions, many areas of A.A. social world activities show spontaneous and rapid change in response to changing makeup of the membership.

For example, there was a marked increase during the 1980s of young people (under thirty-one) in the membership.[14] At the same time, there was also an increase of members abusing other drugs in addition to alcohol (AAWS, 1990).[15] These increases resulted in changes in A.A. activities at the local level. From my experiences in attending many open meetings since the late 1960s, prior to 1970, an acknowledgement of other drug addictions in an A.A. meeting would have been seriously frowned upon. It might even have been suggested informally to those who violated this norm that they belonged elsewhere. However, it became commonplace to hear people introduce themselves as "an alcoholic/addict," or "addict/alcoholic," referring to their dual addictions.[16] Again, as with the increasing number of young people in the meetings, resistance to these changes is still easy to find. But the meeting structure is too loose, permissive and democratic to exclude those with such dual problems, and there is essentially no method by which any restriction could actually be enforced. To paraphrase a comment by a man with over twenty-five years in A.A.,

> It's got so I can't find a meeting anymore without all these kids and "dopers." I don't care what anyone says, it's not the same. I don't see that we have the same disease at all. Why don't they just go to N.A. [Narcotics Anonymous]?

Concerns About Drinking—The Basis for Personal Involvement. Cognitive identification with a particular social world has an underlying basis in some shared interest and/or perspective. This shared interest exists as a precondition, but the identification may arise later as a result of the continued exposure to the ideas, practices, procedures and concerns, which are the foundation of that social world (Unruh, 1983). In the case of A.A., although the cognitive identification which is the basis of membership may not surface until the newcomer has spent considerable time in continued exposure to the activities of the A.A. social world, there is a precondition to this identification which underlies one's personal involvement even prior to such exposure. This is the concern about one's problems associated with drinking.

Whether the newcomer comes to A.A. on his or her own or is sent by others, this underlying concern propels him or her to participate in activities and interactions which introduce others who share that concern. Through the sharing of personal stories and of A.A. values and technology, the cognitive identification is developed. A retired schoolteacher reflected on how she decided to be a member:

> I knew I had a lot of problems and that I drank too much. But I didn't know if I was an alcoholic, or if A.A. was for me. A co-worker gave me A.A.'s Twenty Questions, and I scored pretty high. So I decided to go to a meeting with her. I liked the feeling I got there … and some of the people she introduced me to. So I kept going.
>
> I don't really know what happened next. I guess I kept going and listening for a while. I did read the book, but I didn't get a sponsor yet, because I still didn't think I'd stay. It took about two months to realize

myself what had happened and how much I had already gotten from A.A. That's when I started paying attention in earnest.

Due to the growing expansion of A.A., the lack of spatial contiguity requires that much of the development of knowledge of the A.A. values and technology and the communication of shared interests happen through the use of "linking devices" such as the A.A. literature and other program tools and symbols. These devices will be outlined in the section on dominant modes of interaction.

Principles Before Personalities—The Character of Social Roles. All forms of social organization have both formal and informal social roles. In the social world, these are largely informal. Given the amorphous boundaries and weak authority structure of a social world, "people are not directly controlled, nor do they tend to follow prescribed routes of integration" (Unruh, 1983:37). The formal roles that do exist arise primarily in the voluntary associations and/or formal organizations that comprise the total social world.

So even though the character of social roles in A.A. is generally informal and egalitarian, formal roles exist, although principally in conjunction with the formal organizations within the social world, such as rehabilitation house manager, Alano club treasurer, etc. Formal roles within the meeting structure such as leader or secretary exist primarily for the purpose of the orderly conduct of the meetings themselves, and not to direct or control member activities outside the specific time and place of the meeting. In any case, these roles are basically structured to be weak and not authoritarian. Even the sponsor serves more as a mentor than an authority figure, and the relationship between sponsor and those sponsored is said to be mutually beneficial. A common refrain from sponsors is that: "He has given me as much as I have given him."

Furthermore, even though the Steps offer a prescription for personal recovery, they are offered as suggested only (AAWS, 1976:59), and not enforced. Thus, not everyone follows the same pattern on the path to recovery. For example, a frequently heard discussion among A.A. members involves differences of opinion about the importance of working the Steps "in the order they were written."

Despite the formal effort to maintain an equality of membership, there are those who develop status within the organization, based primarily on years of success in sobriety (old timers, elder statesmen), personal charisma, and/or reputation as a sponsor, speaker, or service worker. These people are sometimes informally referred to as "A.A. gurus." Although the Traditions state that members place "principles before personalities" (AAWS, 1976:564), and newcomers are cautioned against becoming too enamored of such individuals, such people may exert enormous influence and some of them can become quite strict and rigid in directing the recovery programs of others. A particular case in point is that of a well-known southern California circuit speaker[17] whose appearance in any community in that end of the state is an event that packs the house. He also has a reputation as a task master with those he sponsors, exerting considerable direction over their lives, especially during their early sobriety. One interviewee with some knowledge of the Los Angeles groups claimed: "When you don't do it just the way he says, you are berated ... it's just about as close to coercive as A.A. can get."

If the directiveness is too strong, it may drive away some newcomers who are not strong enough to exercise their option to seek out other social world participants with whom to associate. A woman counseling client of mine in her forties, with only a few months of sobriety, stopped going to A.A. for a while after being selected out by a "guru" type at a local Alano club. She explained: "He made me feel as though he were trying to run my whole life."

Nevertheless, such examples of the exerting of personal power tend to be more the exception than the rule, so that it is still fair to emphasize the essential egalitarian nature of A.A. roles in general.

The A.A. Universe of Discourse—Dominant Modes of Interaction. Although face-to-face interaction routinely occurs in the social world, its existence and continuance are primarily dependent on its communication through various media. Through newsletters, books, magazines, bulletins, etc., social worlds "link actors in ways that transcend space" (Unruh,

1983:32). It is true that other forms of social organizations utilize these devices. But in a social world they are vital for the organization.

Media Linking Devices. Again, although face-to-face contact is the dominant mode of communication in A.A. within limited physical or geographic areas, and the group meeting has been the foundation of A.A. personal recovery, the dominant mode of communication that sustains the fellowship at the national and international level is that which is accomplished by the media linking devices that transcend space. Thus communication about the program through its own literature and other media sources has become the foundation of the social world of A.A. For example, it is often asserted that a significant contribution to the initial growth of A.A. was the Jack Alexander article (1941) in the *Saturday Evening Post.* Since then, A.A. has been presented in all areas of the media. Outside the realm of professional publications and in the sphere of popular literature, there are now whole publishing efforts devoted to the market supplied by A.A. and its intersecting worlds. These include Hazelden Educational Materials, *Addiction and Recovery* magazine, and both movie and television productions. "My Name is Bill W." (1989, Warner Brothers Television) was a Hallmark Hall of Fame production for which actor James Woods won an Emmy for his portrayal of Bill Wilson.

The basic literature of the program begins with the "Big Book," referring to the volume *Alcoholics Anonymous,* first published in 1939. This chronicles the start of the movement, lays out the basic principles of recovery and program development, and tells the personal stories of a number of members. It is sometimes referred to as "the Book," which is similar to the way in which the religiously devout may refer to the Bible, and it is a necessary ingredient in the recovery recipe. It is sometimes given as a gift to newcomers who cannot afford one, although the price has remained relatively low, rising from $3.50 at publication to $6.00 in 1989, fifty years later, and more recently to $8.00.

Newcomers are told to "read the Book" every day as part of the prescription, and indeed, many credit this with giving them the beginning of truly deep understanding of their condition, and helping them maintain their recovery even in situations when face-to-face activities are not accessible to them. A former Navy man told me:

> Whenever I was out to sea and there were no members but me, I never lost touch with the program 'cause I read the Book every night, and the *Twenty-Four Hour* book [a small book of meditations widely used by A.A. members]. If it hadn't been for that, I'd prob'ly have been drunk the minute we hit a port![18]

Another important book for the A.A. member is *Twelve Steps and Twelve Traditions*, referred to as "the Twelve and Twelve." This slim volume contains a detailed explanation and interpretation of the program technology, and is generally used as a guide book for conducting "Step Study" meetings, in which participants examine one of the principles in depth and as it relates to problems in their lives. Other books, booklets, pamphlets and materials provide knowledge of A.A.'s existence, its philosophy and technology, packaged to appeal to a wide variety of population groups (e.g. women, teens, family, professionals). Finally, there are newsletters published by local community central committees, and the A.A. worldwide periodical, *The A.A. Grapevine*, which is filled with suggestions for dealing with sobriety and life's problems, as well as A.A. humor. Most A.A. literature can be purchased at meetings, the local service center or by mail. Pamphlet prices may be as low as five or ten cents.

In addition to the literature, items of A.A. jewelry, bookmarks, wallet cards imprinted with the Serenity Prayer, tokens of sobriety, and bumper stickers with A.A. slogans, are available through private enterprises such as specialty bookstores and mail order companies. Although many of these are not officially sanctioned by A.A., and indeed, there have been controversies over the "unauthorized use" of A.A. symbols for some profit-making activities (*Sober Times*, May, 1990; Bishop, 2006),[19] such symbolic items are often given as gifts between members, and serve to identify and foster communication among them outside of A.A. activities. A recent example of this occurred when a professional colleague and A.A. member with over thirteen years in the program was introduced to a woman manager of our company who was wearing a gold pendant with a version of the triangle and circle that is the basis of the A.A. logo. There was instant recognition as he smiled and said: "I sure like your program!"[20]

Face-to-Face Communication. Of course, face-to-face communication remains basic to the A.A. social world. Formally, it occurs at meetings, conventions, and in A.A. service work.

Meetings are organized around a designated speaker or two (Speaker meetings), open sharing on a particular topic (Participation or Discussion meetings) or readings in the "Big Book" or "Twelve and Twelve" (Big Book Study or Step Study meetings). As previously mentioned, some meetings are designated for special populations, such as women only, men only, Spanish-speaking, etc. But all meetings that are not designated as closed, are officially open to any interested persons.[21]

Meetings are routinely opened by the leader with established words of A.A. welcome (*The A.A. Grapevine*, 1947). The format may vary slightly, but some of the rituals may include newcomers and visiting members from other areas being asked to introduce themselves "so we can get to know you better," reading from the A.A. literature,[22] celebrations of milestones in members' recovery (birthdays or anniversaries), and the sharing of personal stories according to the A.A. guidelines of telling "what we used to be like, what happened, and what we are like now." (AAWS, 1976:58). As A.A.'s Traditions state that A.A. groups "ought to be fully self supporting through our own contributions" (AAWS, 1976:564), a basket or other container is passed for donations, and the meeting is closed by the leader.

Although the manner of closing the meeting also has many variations, in southern California it is usually done by the leader asking for "all who care to" to join in a closing prayer. This is done in a hand-clasped circle, and the prayer is most often the Lord's Prayer. At the end of the prayer, those standing in the circle squeeze hands and call out in chorus: "Keep coming back: it works!"[23]

The interactive processes that are incorporated into the formal meeting ritual thus seem to suggest a warmth and camaraderie among members that is often very appealing to newcomers, many of whom are in considerable physical and mental distress. Speakers will often talk about what their first meetings were like. A common assessment follows along these lines:

> I was confused and scared. I don't think I really heard anything that was said that night. But I felt a lot of warmth in the room. And people who talked to me made me feel cared about and accepted. So when I was told to keep coming back, I did.

While participants are not told in an authoritarian manner that A.A. membership is required or that any particular level of ongoing participation is necessary, there are strategic points at which their testimonials reflect that they have come to believe that some level of involvement is necessary for them to maintain their sobriety. One such critical point is following a relapse, or in the midst of a stressful time when temptation to drink is strong, or when plunged into great psychological turmoil (a "dry drunk"). Statements like the following from a woman who relapsed after many years of abstinence are common:

> I got away from the program. I wasn't going to meetings or reading the Book ... lost contact with A.A. people. I was cocky. I forgot how much I needed all of you ... these rooms ... and what goes on here ... my "h.p." [higher power] ... I lost contact with him too.

Such statements are not just confessionals. They serve as points of identification for other members and as warnings that they too could have a "slip"[24] if they stray too far from their A.A. involvement. This is reflected in members' attitudes toward those who leave and go back to drinking destructively. The expression often used in these situations is: "There, but for the grace of God, go I."

There are no set rules as to how many meetings a member should attend or how often. But it is sometimes presented to newcomers as a rule of thumb that if one drank every day, one should go to a meeting every day, at least in the initial phase of recovery. Another rule of thumb is the "90/90 rule," which means 90 meetings in 90 days.

As mentioned, other formal or structured social interactions among members occur through their participation in A.A. service work. Step Twelve specifies that "carrying the message" of A.A. to other alcoholics is an inherent and necessary part of personal recovery. Members fulfill this function through a variety of activities. These include volunteering to answer the phones or staff the local central office, serving on the Central Committee, or the Hospital and Institutions Committee (which conducts meetings and brings A.A. to those who are confined in hospitals and prisons), being leaders or secretaries of meetings, serving as speakers, and assuming other meeting duties such as making coffee or setting up the room. From a middle aged man:

> Doing service was an important part of my feeling like I was part of it all, so to speak. I really resisted at first … you know … too busy and too proud. First I led a couple of meetings, and it felt good. Then I got humble, and made the coffee for a month. Now I am on the H & I (Hospital and Institutions) Committee, and that makes me feel like my sobriety is important, not just to me, but to others as well.

Finally, members may attend regional, state or international conventions, and both small and large local and area conferences, sometimes called "round-ups." At these gatherings there may be speakers brought from other parts of the country, workshops on special topics, and informal hospitality rooms for mingling and conversation. Some conferences are put on by special groups within A.A., such as a women's conference or a gathering of A.A. historians and archivists.[25] At many of these gatherings, there are also meetings for family members, such as Al-Anon and Alateen, thus expanding somewhat into the larger social world of recovery. Therefore, these conventions and conferences are an opportunity for members and often their families as well, to heighten their involvement and commitment to the fellowship and the "A.A. way of life." A long-time member, active in a variety of aspects of the fellowship, who had attended several such events, told me:

> It's nice to see members outside your own area. Once you've gone to a few, it's a way to see people you don't get to see otherwise. There's a warm, friendly atmosphere, like a family reunion, or like "old home week."

Social Life in A.A.

Now that the social world perspective has been established as one from which to view A.A., it is possible to examine aspects of that world that have previously received little attention, such as A.A. social life.

Membership in the social world of A.A. encompasses far more than the acts of members associated with the primary purpose of recovery from alcoholism. It offers an opportunity for a wide range of social interaction and activity. This interaction usually extends beyond the meeting rooms, and is not necessarily limited to activity related to the common problem of alcoholism. It may include everything from coffee klatching at a local coffee shop after meetings to networking for jobs, participation in planned and unplanned recreational activities, sharing living arrangements, establishing friendships, love affairs and marriages.

Even within the formal context of a meeting, there is a great deal of informal exchange both immediately preceding and after the meeting. There is friendly conversation and even embracing as members greet or depart or share feelings about some aspect of the meeting. Depending on whether the meeting is a day or evening meeting, weekday or weekend, members may go off in small friendship groups or cliques to a social setting such as an Alano club, a local coffee shop, a private home, etc., for meals, informal conversation and other joint social activity. The importance of the informal coffee klatch was illustrated by the statement of a young woman in her very early twenties, with two years in the A.A. program:

> I don't think I would ever have been able to hang in there long enough to get the cobwebs out of my brains if it hadn't been for what went on after meetings. I had been used to a lot of late night partying ... and the coffee groups when the meetings were over kept me away from the old drinking and using crowd.

Depending on the size of a particular community, there may be a variety of organized social activities such as picnics, dances, golf tournaments, and camping trips sponsored by a local A.A. committee or one of the cooperating facilities such as a rehabilitation house or Alano club. Family members and friends are welcome at A.A. social events which all take place in a non-drinking environment where all participants are expected to be abstinent from alcohol. The chairperson of an upcoming Alano club "Casino Night," responded to a member's question about bringing her neighbor: "Anyone who's sober and has five bucks is welcome."

Frequently, the experience at an informal social event in a sober environment may make an impact on an individual's grasp of his or her life situation and commitment to recovery. At an A.A. New Year's Eve party held in a large downtown facility in a metropolitan community, about four hundred people were dancing and seeing in the New Year without alcohol. A young man at my table was noticeably pleased, as he explained: "This is only the second time in my life I ever danced when I was sober. I wasn't even sure I could do it!"

In some communities, Alano clubs serve as a hub of social world activity in a given geographic area. One of the clubs from which many subjects for this research were drawn is housed in a large two-story building in a beach community of the city near private homes and small businesses. Upstairs, there is a large meeting room, rest rooms and quarters for the club custodians. Downstairs, there is a large lounge, rest rooms, card room, TV room, and a dining room and kitchen, which constitute a member restaurant.

The club has a membership of over three hundred, among whom are doctors, teachers, scientists, students, service and business people, homemakers, and tradespeople. Many members spend much of their leisure time in the club, playing cards, dining with friends, going to meetings and networking. The club has a bulletin board for members to advertise jobs, rooms for rent, and products to buy or sell, and another for personal messages.[26]

Sometimes, the informal associations become primary in the lives of members, so that meeting attendance falls off, and they may be chided by other members. One man was overheard getting after a friend about his shirking meetings and playing cards too much: "Sometimes, I think your 'higher power' is the gin rummy god!"

So there are also many A.A. members who deliberately shy away from the Alano club scene, feeling that the activities there may be more corrupting than helpful. One long-time member, active in A.A. service work, told me:

> This is somewhat of an exaggeration, but rightly or wrongly, some people see them as places where losers on disability sit around all day and collect government checks ... play cards, try to "thirteenth-step" newcomers, or are just too lazy to go out and get a real job.

Nevertheless, for many, especially those who at first do not take well to or are unable to handle the intense closeness imposed by the meeting, the clubs provide a safe, sober haven from the drinking world, an initial place of comfort within the A.A. world, and an arena for observing the values of participation. As one man in his early forties with fifteen years of sobriety explained:

> For the first two and a half years, I hung around the club, but didn't get involved. Oh, I went to meetings, but I didn't get much better. It was fear and having a place to hang out that kept me sober. But then I started looking at those who were working the program ... their lives coming together ... so I started going to more meetings and got a sponsor.

Relationships in A.A. The only formalized A.A. relationship is embodied in the concept of sponsorship. Considerable attention has been given to this relationship, and it is described elsewhere in this chapter and also in Chapter 4. Little has been written, however, about informal relationships in the fellowship. Despite its loose and somewhat fragmented organizational structure and the fact that face-to-face contact among members is sometimes limited to one's most immediate geographic community, there is a bond among A.A. members which defies barriers of both geographic and social distance. Members who have never seen each other develop an instant rapport as members of A.A. When members visit from other places, they are often applauded at meetings, and interactions among members appear similar to those one might expect among members of a large extended family.[27] In fact, for many members, the fellowship serves as a primary group similar to a family. As a thirty-five year old man put it:

> This is my family now. My folks washed their hands of me a long time ago. I've been through four marriages. I do want to get back with my kids some day. But for now, I get what I need from the people here. They're the ones that taught me how to live.

And from a man in his fifties with over twelve years of sobriety: "I really need to be around A.A. people. This [Alano club] is where I come to be nurtured."

In addition, for other members, it may also function as an introduction service for the development of a wide range of relationships, including romantic attachments. This is sometimes a source of confusion and conflict, especially in close geographically defined communities where members attend meetings throughout that community. A.A. is virtually a "fish bowl" for those who use it in that manner. As one member expressed it: "Sometimes it almost seems incestuous!"

Norms of appropriate dating and mating practices are similar to those in the larger society, and sanctions for violating them reflect some of the same modern permissiveness. In general, sponsoring persons of the opposite sex is proscribed in order to help prevent sexual entanglements, which interfere with recovery. One strongly condemned behavior involves some members preying upon or "hustling" newcomers or those in early sobriety for sexual relationships. This is perceived as exploitative in the sense that newcomers may still be too confused to be able to make responsible choices but are vulnerable to attention and in need of warmth and affection. Yet, so common is this behavior, that it is cynically given the status of an A.A. principle not found among the original twelve. Thus such behavior is labeled "Thirteenth Stepping."

While usually applicable to male members' behavior toward females, this is not always the case. A young man in his thirties with about a year on the program, still subject to periodic depressions, became attached to an

A.A. woman in her forties with several years of sobriety and A.A. involvement. While it was clear to many of her friends that the relationship was not serious for her, the young man became deeply involved and was devastated when she ended it. His depression led him to a brief "slip," and the woman was the subject of some disparaging comments for what some perceived as "Thirteenth Stepping" on her part.

This proscribed behavior notwithstanding, many A.A. members form long-term friendships and love relationships. In fact, there is sometimes a pattern established of serial marriages and divorces within the same A.A. community. This may mean that current and former partners remain a part of one another's ongoing social environment, which means that all of them must redefine their relationship in such a way that all are able to continue their participation in the local A.A. community comfortably, or otherwise one or more will be forced to alter either their geography or level of involvement. Thus, while A.A. relationships may be subject to the same happy endings and heartbreaks as those formed outside the program, in A.A. it is often difficult to find distance from a relationship "gone bad." This was illustrated by the following comment made by a very stylish and attractive female A.A. member of about thirty-five who had been married to four different A.A. men: "It's getting so I can't go to a meeting in this town without running into one of my ex-husbands!"

Other A.A. relationships may be formed on the basis of actual kinship, neighbors, old drinking buddies, co-workers, etc. At one meeting I listened to a man in his early forties tell how he and his brother and sisters had convinced his parents, both of whom had a drinking problem, to come to A.A. A nurse I worked with who was an A.A. member, had two brothers also in A.A., and another woman in A.A., whom I knew well, was able to "Twelve-Step" her own daughter successfully at age eighteen. One of my favorite stories about neighbors in A.A. was told to me by a counselor who worked on a treatment program with me. He had over six years of sobriety at the time, but told the story of his first A.A. meeting which is paraphrased as follows:

They took me to a meeting directly from jail. I was always afraid to go because I'd see someone who knew me there. Sure enough, there was my next-door neighbor! I was hoping he wouldn't see me ... but he came up to me and said, "I was wondering when you would get here." When I asked how he knew, he said, "How could I not know. You've been throwing your empties in my garbage can for three years!"

Intersecting Social Worlds

Strauss' concept of intersecting social worlds (1978) is illustrated by those that are related to A.A. Generally, these are of two types:

1) Those related specifically to the philosophy and format of the A.A. program or to the A.A. movement, and have arisen directly from it, and

2) Those related to the purpose of dealing with the problems of alcoholism and have intense involvement with the social world of A.A., even being strongly influenced or modified by this association.

The first type includes other Twelve-Step programs which copy the wording of the A.A. twelve steps and twelve traditions, with minor verbal variations, and use these as the basis of their attempts to deal with addictive or compulsive problems other than alcoholism. These include groups such as Gamblers Anonymous, Narcotics Anonymous, Overeaters Anonymous and the family programs of Al-Anon, Naranon, Alateen, etc. The second type includes some forms of alcoholism treatment programs, community alcoholism education organizations, including employee assistance programs in the work place and drinking driver education and counseling programs.

A.A. members may be found as participants in one or more of these interacting worlds as either receivers or providers of the services given. Such is the case with a young woman who frequently introduces herself at meetings in the following manner: "My name is Sue and I have all the A's!" (i.e., is in all of the anonymous twelve step programs).

Furthermore, many A.A. members now have their initial contact with A.A. while in a formal treatment program, and many counselors and other staff of these programs are themselves members of A.A.

Ninety-Day-Wonders, Two-Hatters, and Members Employed in Alcoholism Treatment. While it is true that most A.A. members limit their counseling aspirations to Twelve-Step work, an increasing number have been getting into counseling and treatment work. When I began work in the alcoholism field in the late 1960s, there was no alcoholism counseling profession, and few paraprofessionals. Currently, these counselors may be found on the staff of almost every treatment program. They are frequently A.A. or N.A. members, and sometimes it is even specified for the position that they be in recovery or "life-experienced."

As a professional in the treatment field, I often observed patients in treatment and newcomers to A.A. who were so initially enthusiastic about their own sobriety that they expressed aspirations of becoming counselors themselves. In A.A., these people are patronizingly referred to as "ninety-day-wonders,"[28] because a kind of messianic fervor to save others seems to overtake them at about three months into their sobriety. This is viewed with some amusement, but also with some concern that they will quickly burn themselves out worrying about other people's programs instead of concentrating on their own recovery. Furthermore, as a known teacher in the field, I have often been approached in the Alano Club after an A.A. meeting by such A.A. members asking me what courses to take and where to apply for school.

On the other hand, there are those who may already be involved in human service delivery before coming to A.A., or who after some years of sobriety, Twelve-Step work and perhaps volunteer work, decide to develop themselves as professionals, and do so with considerable success. The growth of their numbers is largely attributable to the public funding of programs where insider knowledge of A.A. was needed on the part of counselors. This funding, made possible by the passage of the Comprehensive Alcohol Abuse and Alcoholism Prevention, Treatment and Rehabilitation Act of 1970 (known as the Hughes Act for Senator Harold Hughes, himself a recovering alcoholic), also supported training programs for those people in recovery who did not hold degrees in such professions as psychology, social work, and counseling. Once trained, these A.A and N.A. members could become certified to work in these programs.[29] (Olson, 2003).

Within the context of the A.A. social world, these people originally were referred to as "two-hatters" because they functioned alternately in the roles of members and of providers of professional counseling or recovery services to members. The term has been officially replaced by "members employed in the alcoholism field." However, informally, the term "two-hatters" still persists to some degree.

There are some problems involved for the member who is in this position. In the member role, the relationships between them and other members is egalitarian, while in the counselor role, it is generally more authoritative. Some "two-hatters" have had to juggle their schedules in order to avoid role conflicts at meetings. As one put it:

> I go to meetings with my clients, but I also go to at least one each week far enough away from the hospital to insure I won't see any of them there. There has to be one place where I can feel free to share my stuff and not have to worry about whether or not my having problems is going to undermine my value as a counselor.

Another problem for "two-hatters" is a resentment on the part of some other members who perceive the counselor as getting paid to do Twelve-Step work. Despite A.A.'s official acceptance of such activity and its view that it is not the same as A.A. Twelve Step work by its members (AAWS, 1953:170–171), there is a common misunderstanding that persists. As a forty-year-old businessman with eight years of sobriety expressed it: "They're selling what A.A. gave them for free!"

Thus, while these members have expanded the A.A. sphere of influence and formed the foundation for a new profession, they have also become a subject of some controversy, at least in the informal social world of A.A.

Other Intersecting Social Worlds. In addition to the intersecting worlds of alcoholism treatment and other Twelve-Step programs, members may join with other members in a variety of other worlds of both work and leisure activity unrelated in any way to A.A. One finds members forming groups around such events as duplicate bridge, marathon running, supporting local sports teams, golf tournaments and motorcycle riding, just to name a few. Names given by A.A. motorcyclists to their riding clubs sometimes reflect their allegiances to both social worlds (e.g., "Easy Does It Riders" and "The Fifth Chapter Motorcycle Club"). The Alcoholic Olympics, begun in Los Angeles in the 1970s, became an annual event in both L.A. and San Diego, where it is sponsored by the City Parks and Recreation Department.

Levels of A.A. Involvement

The following sections will describe the variations in A.A. participation according to Unruh's typology of social world involvement, and explain how changes in levels of participation may affect social world integration and successful recovery.

The Pathway to Social World Integration. According to Unruh (1979, 1980), Strangers are naïve in their orientation to the social world, do not know what is going on within it and feel little, if any, commitment to it. Tourists are curious about the social world, but their experiences with it are limited to certain relevant concerns, and commitment is based on some kind of reward. Only as Regulars do people achieve a level of integration into the social world, developing relationships of familiarity and a commitment to its ongoing functioning. Finally, as Insiders, they achieve total identity and act in ways to create the social world for others as well as themselves.

Although there is no prescribed route of integration, it could be assumed that in general, levels of involvement in a social world would follow a progressive, if jerky, course toward such integration. As with A.A., for example, one would begin as a Stranger, without knowledge of the social world other than a remote awareness which is shared with many others in the dominant culture who may not drink at all, or who only drink moderately and without social or health consequences. Once exposed to the philosophy, activities and interests of the social world, some will participate further, but only as Tourists for limited time and purpose. However, others will develop relationships and an interest that will propel them to higher levels of involvement as Regulars and Insiders, thus becoming more and more fully integrated in order to reap the benefits such integration can offer in terms of their recovery. At times this progression may occur rapidly and simultaneously, so that the member becomes both a Regular and an Insider at the same time. At other times it occurs more slowly, perhaps even with some backsliding and then forward surging.

A.A. Newcomers. Based on a perceived need for assistance and program structure in dealing with an alcohol problem, the alcoholic may enter the social world of A.A. on his or her own, or be sent by family, friends, counselor, employer, doctor, clergyman or judge. As one member explained:

> The judge said I had to go to thirty meetings in thirty days, or go to jail for all thirty! I didn't know what I was getting into, but I figured it would be better than jail.

Another means by which the alcoholic Stranger may first come in contact with A.A. is through "recruitment." The Twelfth Step establishes that reaching out to other alcoholics is part of the program of recovery. The beginnings of A.A. are historically traceable to the active participation of the two cofounders in visiting hospitals and inquiring of clergymen in a search for alcoholics to whom they could "carry the message." Although such outreach is part of the program in every community through the work of the Hospital and Institutions Committee and through telephone hot lines and Twelve-Step volunteering in many larger urban centers, the Traditions state that A.A.'s public relations is based on "attraction rather than promotion"(AAWS, 1976:564). This dictates that participation in the recruitment is voluntary on the part of the recruit, and that the content of the message does not involve pressure to become a member, but consists of the telling of the members' own stories in hopes that the recruit will "want what we have" and "be willing to take certain steps" (AAWS, 1976:58). One retired military man explained how one of his shipmates "twelve stepped" him:

> He just talked to me about himself ... told me how he was like me, what he used to do when he drank and how it screwed him up. Then he told me about A.A., and how it had turned his life around. I sure could identify with the mess he had made 'cause I was in one just like it. I really didn't understand much of what he said about A.A., but I could see that he was O.K. now, and I wanted to be that way too.

Strangers or newcomers may not initially consciously perceive themselves as alcoholics or even as having a drinking problem. At meetings, they tend to sit in the back, speaking to no one, perhaps looking anxious, frightened or angry. They tend to have little or no understanding of what is going on. They may of course, choose to remain Strangers and to leave the social world of A.A., whether or not they continue drinking in the same pattern.

The fates of those who leave still as Strangers are unknown, and some may find other routes to recovery. But the statistics on alcohol-related mortality and morbidity remains high.[30] On the other hand, sometimes their problems progress to a point where they eventually return to A.A., perhaps some time later, with different outcomes. As one man in his thirties with about two months of sobriety told it:

> When I first got here, I wasn't ready. I only came to please my wife. I went to a few meetings and I stopped drinking for three weeks. But I didn't really understand what it was all about, and didn't care. I figured I could just stay sober on my own ... and I did too ... for about two more weeks. Then I thought I could handle it ... well you know what happened ... so three years later, and my marriage over, here I am again. This time, I'm here on my own, and I'm really working at it.

On the other hand, some who come to A.A. as Strangers will quickly develop the necessary cognitive identification and rapidly progress to a higher level of involvement. A more detailed explanation of the process by which this occurs is contained in Chapter 4.

In and Out and On the Fringes. Actually, the situation described in the first half of the immediately preceding quote also describes the Tourist in

A.A., a person who participates to satisfy requirements or wishes of others and, less frequently, their own personal concerns, but who have not established a voluntary identification with the organization or a commitment to the program.[31] As one man put it: "I came to get everybody off my back!"

Tourists may minimally take on the role of the member, attending meetings, reading literature, interacting with other members and learning the language. But their attendance and other kinds of involvement remain sporadic, and many of them stop altogether as soon as externally enforced participation ends, and they go the way of Strangers. However, depending on the degree to which they have learned the A.A. technology or formed relationships with members, they may not truly revert to the Stranger role, and may indeed return to A.A. at a time when their alcoholism has progressed, triggering a return of A.A. associations leading to the necessary cognitive identification. A former patient of mine when I worked in an alcoholism treatment facility reported her experience as follows:

> I had gone to a few meetings because my husband insisted I try. But I didn't feel comfortable there. I just didn't think I was that bad. But after five years of more drinking, I was at my wit's end, and so was my husband. I remembered this one girl who really tried to help me, and I found her number. I called, and decided it would be worth another try. As it turned out, it wasn't quite enough, so I had to come to treatment too.

Although the Tourist may not perceive a need for the program, the structure or the supportive interaction, this may be easily perceived by others inside and outside of the social world. Therefore the Tourists' participation in the social world may be such that they are minimally integrated, but are said to be still "in denial." Although no formal pressure is exerted, some members may practice what is sometimes referred to as "tough love" in dealing with these newcomers, similar to that encouraged by programs designed to help parents with difficult adolescents (York, York and Wachtel, 1984). This means that while being supportive of attempts to come to a redefinition of the situation and the work of the program, they are resolute in refusing to accept excuses and alibis from the individual, and they insist on the acceptance of responsibility by that person for his or her own behavior. Following is a paraphrasing of remarks made by a young woman of about nineteen or twenty recently returned to A.A. meetings:

> I wasn't really committed to the program. I kept making excuses. I thought I could stay sober long enough for my folks to let me come back home, then forget about A.A. But my sponsor told me I was playing games. I hated her for not understanding me, but she understood me better than I did myself. I thought she was being too hard on me, but later I found out that was what I needed.

Furthermore, this is sometimes effective without the Tourist having to leave, engage in further drinking for a long period of time, and then come back gravely chastened. Many testimonials from A.A. members who were originally sent to A.A. as part of a court order or a drinking driver program attest to this. The following remark by one young man is somewhat typical:

> The DUI [Driving Under the Influence] program was pretty strict. Going to A.A. four times a week was required. So I made up my mind that even though I didn't want to come, I would serve the sentence, so to speak, and make the best of it. So I listened and read and I found out I really liked it here. I even felt better, and when my head cleared up, I started hearing what I needed to hear.

The Socialized A.A. Member. Once the cognitive identification with the goals of the program is made, the newcomer becomes a Regular. Of course, for some, this is accomplished more quickly than for others. The frequency of actual attendance of Regulars may vary, but they generally attend the same meetings on the same days or nights of the week, one of which meetings is usually referred to as their "home group." They participate in the meeting discussions, demonstrating their commitment to the program, and they are well known as Regulars to other members. They will have read the literature, be conversant in the language, have a sponsor, and have worked or be in process of working the Twelve Steps.

Regulars usually participate in the informal social arena by joining an Alano club or forming friendship groups with other members. Although they maintain involvement in other social worlds of work, family and leisure, they tend to seek out other A.A. members to join them in those activities and sometimes find these mutually supportive relationships becoming necessary to their comfort in those other social worlds as well. This is especially noticed at holiday times when drinking is so prominent in the leisure activities of the larger society. One example is that of a military officer who, after a year of sobriety, complained in the Alano club lounge about having to attend a formal military retirement dinner because he anticipated an extreme level of discomfort in that environment now that he was sober.

> I don't think I'm afraid to go ... it's just that I don't like how it feels being around all that now that I have different values and a different attitude.

Another incident involved a middle-aged woman who returned to the club early from an office Christmas party saying: "It was s-o-o-o-o boring. I guess I just would rather be with A.A. friends."

Regulars may remain at that level as long as a sense of belonging and group connectedness remains and they perceive the need for it to protect their sobriety. It is less likely, but not impossible, that Regulars will "slip." When they do, it may be attributed to the fact that they had not progressed to full program participation. In order to do so, it is necessary to be involved in some form of service, and thus to fulfill some functions of an Insider. The common expression in A.A. with regard to one's obligation to service is that one must "give it away to keep it," referring to the belief (embodied in Step Twelve) that service is crucial to recovery.

Creating the Social World for Others. In A.A., Insiders include those who are or have been in A.A. service work. They are those who serve as the meeting leaders and secretaries, volunteers and organizers of activities, publishers of newsletters, Twelve-Step workers, sponsors, circuit speakers, and committee members. In the broader social world of recovery, they may be Alano club officers and rehabilitation house managers. They create structured social interaction in the formal and informal arenas of discourse.

Meeting speakers, for example, have events organized around them, such as a dinner party. Circuit speakers have especially high visibility, and their personal stories become widely quoted by those who have attended meetings where they spoke, or heard tape or c.d. recordings of them speaking. Just as with professional conferences, there are small commercial operations that go around taping A.A. speakers at main conferences and conventions, and making these recordings available for sale. One young man told me how he used his tapes: "If I can't get to a meeting, I listen to Bob E. or somebody like that. It helps me to keep connected."

In the past twenty-five years or so, celebrities from other social worlds, such as entertainers, sports stars and political figures, have "gone public" with their alcoholism and recovery and have received much media attention.[32] While they have usually respected the A.A. tradition of anonymity where their A.A. membership is concerned, it has been largely assumed from the nature of their stories that they had become part of the A.A. social world. In some A.A. quarters, their violation of personal anonymity, especially at the level of press, radio and other media, has been frowned upon. Yet, their openness may indeed have served a recruitment function. For instance, entertainer Dick Van Dyke, in the film, "Hollywood and Vine" (FMS Productions, 1978), an alcoholism education production, told of total strangers who have written to him to thank him for giving them the courage to face their own alcoholism. But these stars are not usually true Insiders. The real A.A. Insiders remain those in the meeting rooms, central offices and A.A. service facilities who spend hours of their time involved in service work and in creating the social world of A.A. for all its members. Insiders have achieved the highest degree of social world integration.

Variations on the Theme. The progressive step-by-step development of participation is, of course, an idealized model that is rarely fulfilled with complete exactness in the real world. Variations that still follow the linear course include Strangers who go directly to being Regulars or Insiders, or

Tourists who become Insiders at the same time as they become Regulars. However, there are also some variations that do not reflect a progressive integration, and because they do not necessarily result in reduced integration, merit discussion.

Never Again a Stranger. As mentioned previously, it is possible for Tourists to leave the A.A. social world without actually becoming Strangers again. It is virtually impossible for one who has been integrated at the level of Regular or Insider to return to being a Stranger. Even if these people cease to participate in the social world, their experiences, knowledge and understanding of the technology and previous degree of integration remain part of their socialized selves. Those who return to drinking are thought by other members to experience a "cognitive dissonance" (Festinger, 1957) in the drinking world, which it is hoped, will bring them back. They are said to have "a belly full of booze and a head full of A.A."

Trading Places. Furthermore, there are variations in the roles of Tourist, Regular and Insider which allow members who have reached the higher levels of integration to move back to lower levels without losing their basic identification with the social world, their commitment to its continuance or their own personal recovery. These changes are generally brought about because of changing perceptions in the need for A.A. structure or in priorities in relationships and other social worlds of family or work. Examples of Regulars and Insiders who may return to being Tourists are those members described in a previous section who work in the field of alcoholism treatment. A nurse working on an alcoholism treatment unit put it this way:

> Now that I work in the field, the program is a constant in my life all day. In a way, it's great to have all the slogans on the wall, and be where my program is part of my daily work. But in another way, it's enough, and when the day is over, I often don't feel like going to a meeting for more of the same.

A director of an alcoholism treatment program spoke in somewhat similar fashion:

When I got into this work, I dropped off. Still, I have an A.A. marriage and A.A. friends. It's just not all there is anymore. As for meetings, I go to my home group every year to take my cake, and that's about it.

Maintaining a Level of Involvement. While the member may vary participation levels based on the perceived need for the structure or support of the program or situational changes which give priority to the demands of other social worlds, the failure to maintain one's participation in the program, for whatever reason, is the primary A.A. explanation for recidivism into alcoholic drinking. No matter how long one has been sober, there is the belief that failure to continue participating or working the A.A. program can result in being overcome by psychological vulnerabilities or by social pressures of the drinking society, so that the person finally gives in to the delusion that one can drink "normally." An expression in A.A. is that "the farther one is from the last drink, the closer one is to the next." As expressed in the testimony of a fifty-five-year-old woman returning to a meeting after a brief relapse preceded by twenty years of sobriety:

> I thought I had it made. After all, I had been sober longer than I was ever a drunk! I got so complacent about meetings. I didn't need them anymore. But as it says in the Book, the disease is powerful. And all we have to fight with is this program. And when I let that out of my life, it cost me!

Summary and Conclusion

Using Unruh's (1983) typology of social organization features, I have described how A.A. may be viewed from a social world perspective.

In terms of population encompassed, A.A.'s worldwide membership of approximately two million is limited only by the extent to which information and knowledge of its existence is available to those who would identify with its goals and interests. A.A. is not bound by physical location or spatial contiguity, and since membership is not dependent on any formal protocol and there are no membership rolls or formal recognition of membership, the dominant boundary characteristic is the cognitive identi-fication of the people involved.

Since the only requirement for A.A. membership is a "desire to stop drinking," and the identification of alcoholism is left completely to the individual member, A.A. is highly permeable. Furthermore, membership in some aspects of the larger social world of recovery is open to family and friends of alcoholics as well. There are no formal restrictions as to class, race or gender, and membership of women and ethnic minority groups is growing.

The organizational structure of A.A. is that of a "fellowship," rather than an organization in the more traditional sense. Its leaders "are but trusted ser-vants; they do not govern." The organization is a loose association of mem-ber groups linked to the General Service Board of Alcoholics Anonymous, Inc. through local districts and area assemblies whose representative provide input into policy decisions through General Service Conferences. Officially, the General Service Board stands at the top of the organizational structure, and it in turn has two subsidiary corporations, Alcoholics Anonymous World Services (which publishes A.A. books and pamphlets) and The Grapevine, Inc. (which publishes the A.A. monthly periodical).

The broader social world includes formal associations that are specifi-cally related to A.A. such as Twelve-Step rehabilitation houses and Alano clubs. Separate family groups such as Al-Anon and Alateen, Adult Children of Alcoholics and other Twelve-Step programs such as Narcotics Anonymous, Overeaters Anonymous, and Gamblers Anonymous, are based on the A.A. philosophy and technology, and are intersecting social worlds which make up the larger social world of recovery.

Since there is an absence of a strong central authority structure, influ-ence of this structure on the daily lives of the members, except in some of the formal associations such as rehabilitation houses, is weak. Furthermore, the lack of this authority, and of bureaucratic lines and spa-tial limits, means that some aspects of the social world are subject to rapid and spontaneous organizational change. This is reflected in the changes in the makeup of the membership to include more young people and more people with dual or multiple addictions to alcohol and other drugs.

Although members come from diverse personal and cultural backgrounds, they are brought together by their shared concern about alcohol problems. The character of social roles in the A.A. social world is essentially weak and egalitarian, although in some of the formal associations that make up the larger world, there are some individuals who exert somewhat stronger controls, e.g., rehab house manager. Furthermore, some informal roles, such as sponsor or circuit speaker, allow for certain charismatic individuals to develop stronger influences over other members, even though the Traditions and A.A. program folklore caution members against becoming too enamored of such individuals.

Finally, given the growth in the membership and the lack of spatial limits in its sphere of influence, the dominant mode of interaction on which it depends at the higher level of its structure and the broadest dimensions of its scope is through the use of various media "linking devices" such as books, pamphlets, periodicals and various symbols which are even displayed on jewelry and bumper stickers.

Two aspects of the A.A. social world which have also emerged in this study, have had little attention in the literature and are potential areas for further study: those of informal A.A. relationships and of developing intersecting social worlds. The examples given suggest that relationships in A.A. resemble those in an extended family, so that in some instances, the fellowship becomes a family substitute, providing nurturance and re-socialization in the area of basic values.

Using the typology developed by Unruh (1980) of levels of social world involvement, we can frequently see a basically linear progression, where integration into the social world reflects members' movement from Strangers or Tourists to levels of Regulars and Insiders. However, the data also suggests that once full integration has been achieved, members may subsequently move from higher to lower levels of participation without this necessarily affecting social world integration or successful recovery. Nevertheless, some degree of social world integration is necessary for members to become socialized into the A.A. way of life, and therefore to be successful in A.A. recovery.

3

The Social Construction of Group Dependency

As demonstrated in Chapter 2, A.A. recovery is associated with integration into the A.A. social world. While some formal activities are considered core activities, such as attendance at meetings, reading the literature, sponsorship, working the Steps and doing service, there are a variety of ways and different degrees of participation in which successful members combine formal and informal activities to achieve this integration: that is, to move from Stranger and/or Tourist to Regular and Insider. Since much of A.A. activity takes place in a group environment, the extent to which members can and do participate easily within this group orientation is important to the social integration process.

Previous studies have suggested that a high degree of comfort with the group sharing approach of A.A., referred to as affiliative needs and group dependency (Trice and Roman, 1970b), may be a precondition for successful A.A. affiliation. However, given that many are sent—even mandated—to attend A.A. by outside sources, it is likely that there are some who enter the social world who do not fit the psychological profiles described in this literature. This gives rise to several questions, such as: Are those who come to A.A. with low degrees of affiliative needs and group dependency destined to failure as Strangers or Tourists in the social world? Or are there ways in which some of them may also become integrated as Regulars and Insiders? If so, what ways might the experiences that lead to their success be different from those of more group-dependent persons? Is it possible that the degree of affiliative orientation and group dependency may be socially constructed through certain interactive processes that may accompany participation in the social world?

Analytical Framework

Affilative Needs and Group Dependency. Studies by Trice (1957) and Button (1956) suggested that those who successfully affiliate with A.A. have social skills for coping with spontaneous emotion sharing in the small group patterns which characterize A.A., that these people have self-conceptions which are compatible with such sharing, and that they have experienced it in groups prior to coming to A.A. In a later study, Trice and Roman (1970b) tested several propositions related to A.A. affiliation, where affiliation was defined as attending meetings at least twice a week for one year.[33] Among these propositions was that "successful A.A. affiliates are significantly characterized by affiliative needs and group dependency" (Trice and Roman, 1970b:52). Persons with affiliative orientations were described as those who were friendly, responsive to group opportunities, willing to accommodate demands of others in a group, and open to sharing emotions and problems (Groesbeck, 1958, cited in Trice and Roman, 1970b:52). Based on their data from questionnaires, personality inventories with male alcoholics upon hospital admission and eighteen months after discharge, the proposition was supported.

While the study relies heavily on personality inventories,[34] and does not include evaluation of interactive experiences in A.A., the behaviors and self-concepts associated with what is referred to as group dependency and affiliative need can be widely observed in the A.A. social world. The atmosphere of A.A. activity as described in Chapter 2, is one of intense bonding, sharing of feelings and concerns, emotional support and even physical affection, sometimes with otherwise total strangers. It seems logical that comfort with this environment would be needed for people who enter as Strangers or Tourists to remain and participate long enough to become integrated at the higher levels as Regulars and Insiders.

Yet at any A.A. activity, one also observes those who appear to be outside the mainstream: those who stay to themselves or interact with only one or two others, sitting off to the side or in the back of the room at meetings, participating or "sharing" reluctantly in both the formal meeting and the informal camaraderie. These members do not demonstrate affiliative inclinations, and as the data will show, do not perceive themselves as joiners or as group oriented when they enter the A.A. social world.

The Social Construction of Reality. The process of alcoholism recovery in A.A. requires changes in values, attitudes and beliefs that one may have held since childhood. These changes may be seen as a part of a process of adult re-socialization. To explain the nature of re-socialization, Berger and Luckman (1966) first assert that human reality is constructed in the process of sharing everyday life with others.

Persons are not born as members of society. They are born with the "predisposition to sociality" (Berger and Luckman, 1966:119). The ongoing process of socialization involves both objective and subjective reality and is a dialectic in which the individual interacts with society to establish himself or herself as a member of that society (Berger and Luckman, 1966:119). Berger and Luckman differentiate between primary and secondary socialization mainly on the basis of the affective or emotionally charged nature of relationships with significant others in primary socialization, whereas those in secondary socialization are characterized by formality and anonymity. Both primary and secondary socialization involve cognitive learning, but in primary socialization, the processes are based on the mediation of the world by significant others, which is automatic. In secondary socialization they are based on pedagogic techniques mediated by those in institutional roles (such as teachers).

Primary socialization ends when "the concept of the generalized other has been established in the consciousness of the individual" (Berger and Luckman, 1966:126). Secondary socialization is required to take society beyond the "very simple stock of knowledge" that is "generally relevant" and to develop the specifications of the various sub-worlds that establish and maintain divisions of labor and contribute to human progress. In secondary socialization—which can occur only after primary socialization has taken place—it is sometimes necessary to develop techniques that will enforce learning despite obstacles created by primary socialization. For example, a teacher must use persistence, and make material vivid and relevant to structures already present in the "home world" (Berger and Luckman, 1966:131).

In re-socialization the "processes resemble primary socialization because they have radically to reassign reality accents and, consequently, must replicate to a considerable degree the strongly affective identification with the socializing personnel" (Berger and Luckman, 1966:144). They are different from those in primary socialization in that they do not start from the beginning, and therefore must also involve "dismantling and disintegrating the preceding nomic structure of subjective reality" (Berger and Luckman, 1966:144). The prescription for such re-socialization must include both social and conceptual conditions:

> The most important social condition is the availability of an effective plausibility structure … that is, a social base serving as the "laboratory" of transformation. This plausibility structure will be mediated to the individual by means of significant others with whom he or she must establish strongly affective identification.

There is a reorganization of the conversational apparatus wherein the "partners in significant conversation change." (Berger and Luckman, 1966:145–146)

It is pointed out that the historical prototype of re-socialization is found in religious conversion. A framework of religious conversion will be utilized in Chapter 4 to examine the "transformation of self" (Thune, 1977; Rooney, 1985) that occurs in the successful A.A. member. However, in the following sections, the Berger and Luckman prescription for re-socialization will serve as a framework for examining the way in which A.A. members may develop some perception of affiliative needs and new behaviors more reflective of group dependency in order to successfully integrate into the social world of A.A.

The Social Construction
of Group Dependency in A.A.

Initial Exposure to the Social World of A.A. It is likely that most people will feel somewhat socially distant as Strangers during the initial phase of exposure to the activities of a given social world, especially if they do not have connection to someone who is already a member. In addition, some who first come to A.A. may be experiencing some physical discomfort or mental disorientation that accompanies early sobriety, which may limit their responsiveness.[35] Thus it may be expected that A.A. newcomers and members with low affiliative and group dependency needs would display similar behaviors, e.g., arriving and leaving quietly just as the meeting starts or ends, sitting off to the side or in the back of the room, looking lost or isolated and speaking only as it seems necessary for structural accommodation.[36]

However, once exposed to the setting and the process, those with characteristics described as affiliative in orientation and reflective of group dependency will most likely not waste much time in this position. They will soon be seen engaging in conversation and social interaction with others in the group and increasing their participation in various aspects of the social world. A forty-three-year-old woman with four years of sobriety described herself as always having been a "caring, nurturing" person:

> I am a "people" person … I need people. I really immersed myself into
> the program … started reaching out … and I was open to the meetings
> and to other newcomers.

And from a man of thirty-six, sober fourteen years, who described himself as "friendly and open":

> When I was in jail, I was impressed with the guys who brought the
> meeting in. I didn't affiliate with A.A. right away, but when I did, I did
> it all the way. I went to a lot of meetings and met all kinds of people. I
> liked the look in the people's eyes.

Self-Perceptions of Non-Affiliators. On the other hand, there are those who continue to remain distant from group interaction through many weeks, months and even years. They do not display the behaviors of the group-dependent person. For them, the group is uncomfortable, even frightening. From a sixty-year-old woman with eight years in A.A.: "I was terrified of all those people. But I went because I was about to lose my job."

These people express strong self-conceptions as non-affiliators, "loners," and even misfits. From the same woman: "I was insecure, a loner. I didn't feel like I belonged." And from a thirty-nine year old man with nine years of sobriety: "I mostly drank alone ... in a corner of the bar."

Although people who enter A.A. with a strong group orientation may also leave or require more than one entry to progress beyond the Stranger or Tourist level, the non-affiliators are more likely to drop out because of discomfort felt in the highly social surroundings. One man in his late fifties who had been in and out of A.A. over a five-year period before he had finally put together three years of sobriety told me:

> I never got past feeling like an outsider in those big meetings. I kept going until I'd met the requirement for the judge, but when there was no reason for me to go back, that was the end of it ... until the next time I got into trouble.

And from a woman in her forties:

> I just wasn't into all that hugging and such. It was more comfortable at home by myself. Of course, that kept getting me back to drinking!

Although many of those who leave, as suggested by these examples, do return when their drinking worsens or they are sent again, clearly their integration into the A.A. social world is a more difficult process than for those who are comfortable with the group format, and they may still drop out at any point in the process, even after they have become Regulars. An example of this was illustrated in a conversation I had at an Alano club with one long-time member about another member who, after eighteen years sober, drank again for about six years, and recently had died of alcoholism.

The A.A. member said, "During the last six years, he was in and out. He would go to treatment, but stay only a few days, then leave."

"When I first came to this club," I responded, "I'd see him playing cards a lot. He seemed aloof."

The long-time A.A. member agreed with my assessment: "He went to a few meetings at first, but not much after that. He hung around here, but he never really got close to anyone."

Of the non-affiliators who remain, some continue to behave in an isolated manner, and may even be downright unfriendly. For example, there was one well-known member of the local A.A. community, who despite about twenty years of abstinence from alcohol, attendance at many meetings and even engaging in sponsorship of newcomers, was known throughout the community as "Mean Bill," because of a constantly sour expression, shortness with people and a somewhat demeaning attitude.

The motivation for these people to remain affiliated and to participate even minimally seems to be one of the greater fear. That is, their fear of drinking and/or its consequences is more powerful than their fear of the group. From a sixty-year-old man with eleven years of sobriety:

> I got very ill physically. I had to do something. I went there, but I sat alone for a long time. I didn't feel comfortable. But I was afraid I'd drink again, and it would kill me.

On the other hand, some not only remain to become Regulars, but also seem to change in terms of the comfort and ease with which they are able to participate in the group, even becoming Insiders, helping to create the social world for others. It is the process by which this occurs that I refer to as the "social construction of group dependency," and which is described in the sections that follow.

Making the One-to-One Connection. While some of those with low group affiliative needs and group dependency said they had a "safe" feeling from the non-judgmental acceptance of the group, the most significant event which began their process of integration was making a one-to-one connection with another member. A forty-year-old man with ten years in A.A. told me:

> I went because I had three 502's [DUI offenses] in a year and a half. The first year or so, I just went to meetings, didn't do anything else ... a little reading. I wasn't impressed. They were just people to me. Then I met Judy [now his wife]. We fought a lot about the program and my getting a sponsor and working the Steps.

And from another forty-year-old woman with five years sobriety:

> I was afraid I wouldn't know anyone. They were all strangers, and I wouldn't be accepted. But I forced myself to keep going so I wouldn't drink. Then, one night, this older woman came up and hugged me and said "I love you!"

Often it was this initial connection that seemed to open the way for breaking through the resistance to really giving one's attention to what was going on. As a young man in his thirties, sober three years, told me: "My sponsor told me to go to five meetings a week, to keep my mouth shut and my ears open. I trusted him, so that's what I did." And the thirty-nine-year-old man who described himself as drinking alone in the corner of the bar explained: "My boss's husband was in A.A. She brought us together, and he was the one who got me to start listening."

Thus, while there may have been resistance to linkage with the group, the development of a dyadic significant-other relationship served as an initial impetus for beginning the process of integration.

Hearing One's Story. The giving of attention also set the stage for another significant event, that of hearing things in the life stories of others that were part of one's own. From the woman cited previously who had been hugged by the older member:

> A man I met told me that if I didn't think I belonged, I should hang around, and I would hear my story. Then a few weeks later, this girl got up and as she spoke, it started to dawn on me ... I was so engrossed ...

every word she said I could relate to where I had come from. Here was this woman with seven or eight years in the program telling my story!

Furthermore, by paying attention to what was being said at meetings and perhaps reading some of the literature, some individuals begin to absorb an understanding of the values and the language which, in turn, facilitates an ability to participate in the new conversational structure and allows them to feel more comfortable in developing other dyadic relationships within the social world. As expressed by another man in his forties with over fifteen years of sobriety:

> Once I felt like I knew more about what was going on, I felt better about talking to someone if they came up to me. But I still couldn't make the first move or talk to a group of people.

And again from the man who drank alone in the bar: "The first year, my socializing outside of meetings was with one person at a time."

Sometimes these dyadic relationships remain the core of recovery for non-affiliative types. For example, this was the case with the sixty-year-old man who had stayed sober eleven years, but said that he did so only because of physical problems. As he explained:

> I only go to about a meeting a month anymore. Believe it or not, I have never read the Book. I only worked the first three Steps. I go to the Club, play cards with one or two people … it's the sober environment … and knowing I'm not the only one, and that I can live without it. Joe helped me a lot too. He said if I could make it three years, I'd probably be O.K. I made that by doing whatever he said.

Dismantling Previous Attitudes and Beliefs. The dominant cultural value system regarding drinking reinforces consumption, but places sanctions to some degree against excessive use. The primary emphasis is on self-control, and it is assumed that all persons have this "will power." In the new reality of A.A., this belief system must be dismantled before the alcoholic is ready to accept his or her alcoholism and engage in the behaviors of an A.A. member. This may start with hearing and reading certain passages from the A.A. literature. For example, Chapter 3 of the Big Book explains the A.A. concept of alcoholism:

> We alcoholics are men and women who have lost the ability to control our drinking. We know that no real alcoholic ever recovers control. All of us felt at times that we were regaining control, which led in time to pitiful and incomprehensible demoralization (AAWS 1976:30).

The chapter goes on to give examples of common unsuccessful efforts to drink normally so that readers can quickly diagnose themselves (AAWS, 1976:31). In Chapter 4, the process of redefining alcoholism as a disease is explained in more detail.

Furthermore, in Chapter 5 of the Big Book, a portion of which is often read at meetings, the alcoholic is told that there must be a complete negation of previous ideas and is cautioned: "Some of us tried to hold on to our old ideas, and the result was nil until we let go absolutely" (AAWS, 1976:58). It goes on to describe how the A.A. program works.

The impact of this literature on some of these non-affiliators is demonstrated by the man in his forties who was unimpressed by the people at meetings:

> At first I didn't know I was alcoholic. I didn't stand when they asked for newcomers. But it was hearing Chapter 3 over and over … at some point, maybe … even not at a conscious level … it became clear to me … in about three months. But I still couldn't get Chapter 5 yet. That came much later.

The first three Steps address the dismantling of the belief in one's own power to control one's alcoholism, and offer the A.A. alternative:

> 1. We admitted we were powerless over alcohol—that our lives had become unmanageable.

> 2. Came to believe that a Power greater than ourselves could restore us to sanity.

3. Made a decision to turn our will and our lives over to the care of God *as we understood Him.* (AAWS, 1976:59)

The alcoholic must also dismantle negative self-concepts that he or she has adopted from the knowledge of harm his or her drinking has done to others and the negative labeling and control strategies imposed by society.[37] The basic A.A. methodology for this is to encourage full disclosure of these "wrongs" in order to have them demystified, after which they can be righted by "making amends" and embarking on a more spiritual path. This process is embodied in Steps Four through Twelve, which involve taking personal inventory, making an honest disclosure to oneself, God and another person, making amends, improving one's contact with one's spiritual "higher power," and helping others:

4. Made a searching and fearless moral inventory of ourselves.

5. Admitted to God, to ourselves, and to another human being the exact nature of our wrongs.

6. Were entirely ready to have God remove all these defects of character.

7. Humbly asked Him to remove our shortcomings.

8. Made a list of all persons we had harmed, and became willing to make amends to them all.

9. Made direct amends to such people wherever possible, except when to do so would injure them or others.

10. Continued to take personal inventory and when we were wrong promptly admitted it.

11. Sought through prayer and meditation to improve our conscious contact with God *as we understood Him,* praying only for knowledge of His will for us and the power to carry that out.

12. Having had a spiritual awakening as the result of these steps, we tried to carry this message to alcoholics, and to practice these principles in all our affairs. (AAWS, 1976:59)

Even those who are not disposed toward group affiliation and do not fit the profile of group-dependent persons may find themselves deeply involved in "working the Steps" because of pressure applied by just one person, especially a sponsor. Carrying out the activities specified by the Steps can then sometimes lead a non-affiliative person into a stronger and deeper commitment to A.A. As expressed by another man in his early forties, this man with fifteen years in A.A.:

Working the Steps was what brought me to a belief in a higher power. When I got that, about three years after coming here, that was the start of my real recovery ... I began to *belong* to this program.

And from another woman in her thirties, this one sober about five years:

As I read the Book and started doing the Steps with my sponsor, I felt better ... even though times were still kind of a mess in my life. I felt more spiritual ... better about me.

Taking Chances. After becoming involved in regular attendance at meetings, getting a sponsor, and working the Steps, a next logical step in the process of integration would be doing service work. Generally, this will involve some ability to relate to a group and/or a display of characteristics such as friendliness, openness and responsiveness to others. Even after some months of attendance, self-described non-affiliative types had difficulty with this and were resistant. Nevertheless, based on the trust they had in a particular significant other, such as a sponsor, some would take the chance if so "instructed." From a young man in his late twenties, after leading his first meeting:

> I dreaded it. I tried to get out of it. But my sponsor said it would be good for my sobriety, and so I did what he told me. It wasn't so bad.

And from a fiftyish woman:

> I kept saying I was too busy with my job and family, but she [my sponsor] knew I was hiding behind that. She kept pushing me to volunteer for something. So when the secretary job came open … well, she was sitting there nodding at me. So I said I'd do it.

This same kind of basic socialization process also applies to establishing oneself as a member of the group in an informal sense. Again from the man who was unimpressed at first by the people at meetings:

> I wanted so much to be like my sponsor that I decided to follow in his footsteps and do whatever he did. So I made myself go around at meetings shaking hands with everyone there!

Furthermore, as with the young man at the New Year's Eve dance who was excited about his ability to dance when sober (previously cited in Chapter 2), even the smallest taste of success could be a source of considerable pride and newfound self-esteem. The man who had led the meeting on his sponsor's instruction added: "It made me feel like I might be able to do some things I never thought I could do before."

On the other hand, for some non-affiliators, difficulties remained strong in certain areas, such as the physical contact that is often observed after meetings and other times when A.A. members come together. A young man who pulled away from an older woman who wanted to hug him told me: "I just can't do that."

Some people who had a difficult time with group activities were able to compensate by finding other less personally threatening ways of relating that still accomplished the degree of participation necessary to be viewed and to view themselves as a contributing member of the group: e.g., cleanup after meeting, coffee making, clerical tasks, and other services that required a minimum of interpersonal contact.

Finally, in some cases, members who once perceived of themselves and behaved as isolated and fearful, had become social world Insiders, participating in group activities, even at leadership levels. For example, a woman in her forties once fearful of going to a meeting had become a telephone volunteer for the local central office: "I can't believe how much I like talking to people. I never thought I would!"

And the thirty-nine-year-old man who drank alone in bars had become a treatment program counselor and member of the local Alcoholism Council Board of Directors: "Once, I thought I would die just to have to get up in front of a group and say my name. Now I even hold my own as a professional!"

Perceiving the Need to Belong. For many non-affiliators in this sample of A.A. members, the process described seemed to lead to a new sense of belonging, which in turn created the perception that it perhaps had always been there, but had been "denied" because of fears that it would not be satisfied or because they did not have the skills to develop those interactions. Again from the man who became the counselor and council board member: "I'm still not an extrovert. But now I think I always wanted to belong. I just didn't know how."

The process of socially constructing group dependency and affiliated need that characterizes the experiences of many of these non-affiliators is outlined in Figure 1.

Figure 1

A.A. Integration of Persons with Low Degree
of Affiliative Need and Group Dependency

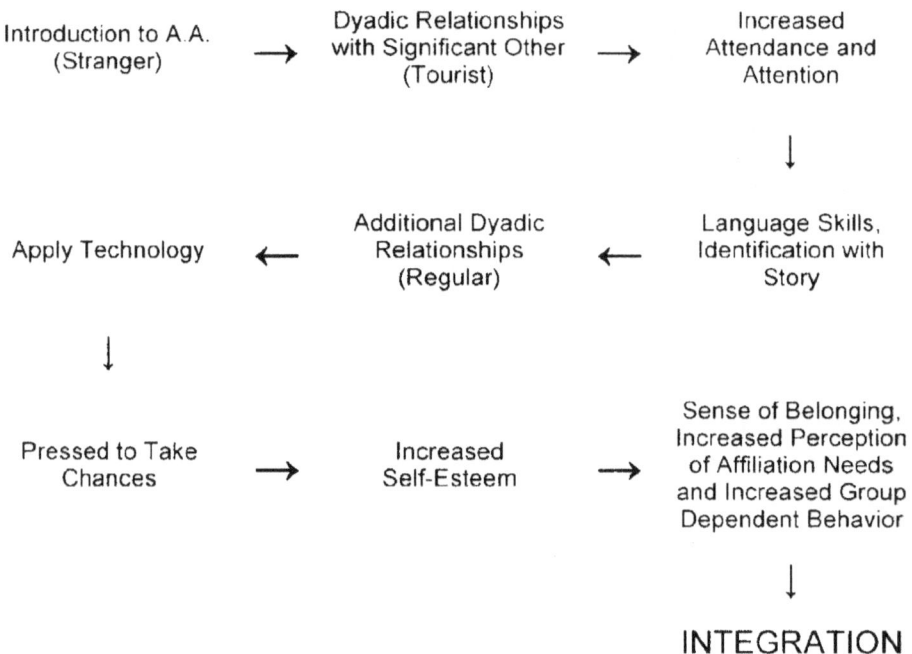

INTEGRATION

Summary and Conclusion

In this chapter, I have illustrated the process by which persons who enter the social world of A.A., but do not fit the profile of persons with high degrees of affiliative need and group dependency may nevertheless, become integrated into the social world and experience A.A. success.

These individuals enter A.A. because of the perception of a drinking problem and an awareness that A.A. helps to deal with such a problem, whether they come on their own or are sent by others. However, because they are uncomfortable in the group setting and in sharing personal information, they do not progress from low levels of participation as easily or in the same manner as those who have high degrees of affiliative need and group dependency. They perceive themselves as misfits and loners, and behave in non group-dependent ways, e.g., continuing to be isolated and even sometimes unfriendly, or leaving the social world completely.

However many of them are able to become fully integrated through an interactive process of re-socialization that seems to begin with the formation of a dyadic significant-other relationship. This relationship often propels them into greater attention to the program content and involvement with the program technology. Increased knowledge of the social world enhances their comfort in forming other significant-other relationships and eventually makes it possible for them to take some chances, especially if "instructed" to do so by significant others. Successes in taking these chances, however minor, seem to enhance self-esteem and lead to further commitment to the social world.

4

A.A. Conversion

Conversion and Self-Transformation

The experience of A.A. members in achieving their recovery has sometimes been described as similar to a sort of *religious conversion* (e.g., Gellman, 1964; AAWS, 1976; Kurtz, 1979; Chesnut, 2006) or *transformation of self* (Thune, 1977; Maxwell, 1984; Rooney, 1985; Denzin, 1987) in which members come to redefine themselves within their life situations, taking on a new self concept, a new role definition, and new values and norms regarding not only drinking, but other social behavior as well. Furthermore, once the conversion is complete, A.A. members gain a "sense of coherence" (Antonovsky, 1980) about themselves and the world, a belief that all will turn out well in accord with the design of one's "higher power."

Central to the A.A. approach is the acceptance of oneself as alcoholic. This involves more than the mere acceptance of a label or the fact that one has alcoholism. It is experiencing at the deepest level of one's existence that one is alcoholic, and therefore can never *not* be alcoholic. It is with this understanding that the alcoholic can grasp the futility of previous attempts to drink like other people and know that only through a total change in attitude toward self and world can he or she remain abstinent, and therefore survive. The process by which this transformation occurs constitutes what may be called the A.A. conversion.

Despite insights provided into member experiences (e.g. Maxwell, 1984) and efforts to establish patterns of A.A. careers (e.g., Leach and

Norris, 1977; Rudy, 1986), questions still remain regarding the process of this transformation. For example, how do the social interactions and experiences in the social world of A.A. relate to the conversion? How do such factors as personal characteristics of participants and the nature or level of social world involvement affect success?

It is the purpose of this chapter to explore answers to these questions by examining four stages of the A.A. conversion career, illustrating the types of conversion experiences characteristic of each of those stages.

Analytical Framework

Religious Conversion Motifs. Lofland and Skonovd (1981) define conversion according to Travisano as "radical reorganization of identity, meaning, life." (Travisano, 1970:594 quoted in Lofland and Skonovd, 1981:375) Rather than focusing on the organizational activities that attempt to bring about conversion, they study it from the perspective of the individual convert. From their research into such experiences, they assert that there are several major types of conversion, and present a typology of six major conversion motifs. Each of these is identified by "what is most memorable and orienting to the person 'doing' or 'undergoing' personal transformation … aspects that provide a tone to the event, its pointedness in time, its positive or negative content and the like." (Lofland and Skonovd, 1981:374)

The six major conversion themes or motifs are identified as the Intellectual, the Mystical, the Experimental, the Affectional, the Revivalist and the Coercive. Major variations by which Lofland and Skonovd distinguish these motifs are:

1) Degree of social pressure to convert

2) Temporal duration of the conversion experience

3) Level of affective arousal accompanying it

4) Affective content of the experience

5) Order in which the individual "adopts a religion's framework and actually participates in its ritual and organizational activities" (1981:376).

The Intellectual motif involves the

Individual, private investigation of possible "new grounds of being," alternate theodicies, personal fulfillment, etc., by reading books, watching television, attending lectures and other impersonal or "disembodied" ways in which it is increasingly possible sans social involvement, to become acquainted with alternative ideologies and ways of life. In the course of such reconnaissance, some individuals convert themselves in isolation from any actual interaction with devotees of the respective religion (1981:376).

This mode of conversion reflects the lowest possible degree of social pressure, takes some time for investigation, and has a moderate degree of affective arousal, with the content of the affective experience being one of "illumination." Furthermore, the conversion is seen to occur before participation in the rituals.

The Mystical motif is, historically speaking, the best-known religious conversion motif. The Mystical conversion is characterized by expressions of a common feeling among converts that "the experience cannot be expressed in logical and coherent terms; [that] characterizations ... miss its depth" (Jules-Rosette, 1975 cited in Lofland and Skonovd, 1981:377).

It is generally associated with a sudden, brief and intense subjective experience. Furthermore, it is characterized by seeming "not to be wrought by the subject, but upon him" (Lofland and Skonovd, 1981:377). Again, there may be little social pressure involved, and the time is brief.[38] Affective arousal is high, perhaps even ecstatic, and the affective content is one of awe, perhaps even fear.

The Experimental motif is probably in reality the most common.

Recent research is uncovering the surprising degree to which ... and the frequency with which ... a transfer of religious identification, behavior and world view can occur quite tentatively and slowly, and yet be identified by the convert-in-process as happening in that manner (Lofland and Skonovd, 1981:378).

This mode represents the pragmatic approach to conversion, in which the convert enters with the attitude of "show me." Social pressure is low, the duration of the conversion is of some time, the affective arousal is low and its content is one of curiosity. Finally, belief follows participation. In the Experimental mode, the first step is learning to act like a convert, with genuine conviction to develop later.

In the Affectional motif, "personal attachments or strong liking for practicing believers is central to the conversion process" (Lofland and Skonovd, 1981:380). The cognitive element is de-emphasized, in contrast to the Intellectual and Experimental motifs. There is a moderate degree of social pressure, the time factor is drawn out, the level of arousal is moderate, and belief follows participation.

In the Revivalist motif,

> Events and activities have an exciting quality. Participants experience emotional heights without suffering subsequent letdowns. There is a promise of more ... the next event, the next day, the coming week. (Taylor, 1978:107 quoted in Lofland and Skonovd, 1981:381)

The process of conversion is brief and intense with ecstatic arousals of love, awe, fear, joy and even guilt, and a high degree of social pressure.

Finally, the Coercive motif "takes place only in extremely rare and special circumstances." It is also variously labeled "brain-washing," "programming," and "mind control" (Lofland and Skonovd, 1981:381). As with the Revivalist motif, belief follows participation, the degree of social pressure is high, as is the level of affective arousal. But the primary affective content is fear, and the temporal duration of the experience is long.

Table 2 illustrates a comparison of these motifs in accord with the five dimensions and is similar to the chart used by Lofland and Skonovd.

Table 2

Religious Conversion Motifs

	(1) Degree of Social Pressure	(2) Temporal Duration	(3) Level of Affect	(4) Affective Content	(5) Belief-Participation Sequence
Intellectual	low or none	medium	medium	illumination	belief → participation
Mystical	none or little	short	high	awe, love, fear	belief → participation
Experimental	low	long	low	curiosity	participation → belief
Affectional	medium	long	medium	affection	participation → belief
Revivalist	high	short	high	love + fear	participation → belief
Coercive	high	long	high	fear + love	participation → belief

These motifs will provide a framework for understanding the process of the A.A. conversion, which I have divided into four stages.[39]

Stages of the A.A. Conversion Career

The following four stages are based on perceived milestone periods in the A.A. conversion career:

Stage I. Entering the Social World of A.A.

Stage II. Establishing the Belief that Alcoholism is a Disease

Stage III. Taking the Role of the Member

Stage IV. Reaching the Moment of Truth

It will also be shown that these stages encompass the various levels of participation or integration into the social world of A.A. from Stranger to Tourist to Regular and Insider.

Stage I—Entering the Social World of A.A.

This stage begins when one is first introduced to the social world of A.A. The level of integration is that of a Stranger, where there is virtually no knowledge or commitment to that social world.

Reflections of three conversion motifs can be identified in this stage of the A.A. Conversion career. These are the Coercive, the Intellectual and the Affectional.

Application of the Coercive Motif. Although membership in A.A. is voluntary, most people do not come to it voluntarily. Often the destructive pattern of their drinking has reached a point where they are sent by a judge, employer, counselor, health practitioner or long-suffering family member, under threat of potential imprisonment, loss of job, health, family or love relationship. As one fortyish man told it: "The judge said I had to go to thirty meetings in thirty days or go to jail for all thirty!" And from a woman in her sixties: "My doctor was the one who said I'd better try A.A. and save what liver I had left!"

In addition, the redefinition of self from drinker to *recovering alcoholic* rarely occurs prior to participation in the program's activities.[40] Indeed, the initial position of the alcoholic regarding acceptance of this label is commonly referred to as one of "denial."[41]

At first glance, this would seem to suggest that many A.A. conversions would follow the lines of the Coercive motif. However, despite the initial social pressure to attend meetings and the fact that participation precedes conversion, the association with this motif stops at the entrance. A.A. itself does not provide the interactional setting necessary to fulfill this type of conversion, and the "brainwashing" approach is not reflected in the life stories of the members.[42] Indeed, the voluntary nature of the program is reflected in its recruitment and public relations policy, which is one of "attraction, rather than promotion" (AAWS, 1976:564), and in the somewhat elitist, even seductive language of its appeal: "If you have decided you want what we have and are willing to go to any length to get it—then you are ready to take certain steps" (AAWS, 1976:58).

Furthermore, once the conversion has taken place, there is neither hatred nor reverence for those who first insisted on it, as one might expect in the Coercive mode. Instead, over and over, one hears expressions of simple gratitude. A man in his late thirties explained:

> Today I can say that I am really grateful to that judge who sent me here. At first, I really resented him for telling me I had to go. But now I see he may have saved my life.

Thus, the application of the Coercive motif, even in the initial stage of the A.A. conversion, is extremely limited.

Application of the Intellectual Motif. At this initial stage, there is still likely to be strong resistance to the alcoholic label as well as to the behavioral norms of A.A. The same young man told me:

> To me, A.A. was a place for scroungy old men who walked around skid row with wine bottles in brown paper bags! That's what an alcoholic was ... and it wasn't me!

This also suggests that the conversion modes in A.A. would not include either the Intellectual or the Mystical types, since in these motifs, belief precedes participation, and the conversion occurs in isolation of social interactions which may lead to it. Nevertheless, despite the variance with the Lofland and Skonovd (1981) formulation, there are some elements of both these types in the actual experiences of members.[43] For example, there are members whose entry into A.A. was indeed preceded by some independent investigation, as in the Intellectual motif, especially if they are among those with higher levels of education who are accustomed to intellectual pursuits. An example of this was encountered in one of those interviewed in an earlier study (Smith, 1986). Bob was a man in his mid-fifties who had been sober for about two years. He had degrees in both engineering and business, and claimed that he had not even been a heavy drinker much before his late twenties.

> I was in my early thirties when I began to realize that I was drinking too much. I began to read everything I could get my hands on, medical stuff, psychology, all of it about alcoholism. I was also interested in religion ... you know ... comparative religions, philosophy and so on. Anyway, I had figured out that I was alcoholic long before I ever got here. For me, it was just a matter of convincing me that I wasn't too good to be one of these people!

Furthermore, although this kind of pre-participation redefinition of self is not the usual, there are also elements of the Intellectual motif in both Stage II and Stage III of the conversion career, as I shall describe in the sections on those stages.

Application of the Affectional Motif. This type of conversion is also evident in the initial stage of conversion. Often those people who do come to A.A. voluntarily still do not do so because they have accepted the alcoholism label, but because of an affectional tie to someone else who has. (This Affectional motif will also be seen to be a key element in Stage III.)

A forty-five-year-old woman with fifteen years of sobriety told me of her first A.A. experience: "No way was I an alcoholic! But G., my boyfriend, was. And he was going, so I did too!" And in my interview with a twenty-eight-year-old man five years sober, he explained: "A friend was in A.A., and she had stopped drinking completely, and was really doing well. I didn't think I was alcoholic, but I knew I should drink less. So when she suggested I go, I did."

Table 3 shows the three conversion motifs which are in evidence during the first stage of the A.A. conversion: Intellectual, Affectional, and Coercive. The other three motifs (Mystical, Experimental, and Revivalist) tend to be completely or almost completely absent at this stage in A.A. as it is practiced in most places today.

Table 3

Stage I Conversion Motifs

	Intellectual	Affectional	Coercive
(1) Degree of Social Pressure	low or none	medium	high
(2) Temporal Duration	medium	long	long
(3) Level of Affect or Emotion	medium	medium	high
(4) Affective/ Emotional Content	illumination	affection	fear
(5) Belief-Participation Sequence	belief → participation	participation → belief	participation → belief

Stage II—Establishing the Belief that Alcoholism is a Disease

Before describing the process involved in this Stage, it seems important to clarify the use of the term "disease" in this context.

The word "disease" appears only three times in the A.A. Big Book. It is mentioned first on page 64 in discussing alcoholism, then again at the beginning of the second part of the book in the story of Bill Dotson, the Akron lawyer who was Alcoholics Anonymous Number Three. When Bill Wilson and Dr. Bob visited Dotson in the hospital, they told him he had "a disease," and when he explained his conversion to his wife, he told her he felt that God had cured him "of this terrible disease." (AAWS, 1976: 187–188, 191)

However, in spite of its avoidance of the specific word "disease," alcoholism is referred to over and over again throughout the book as a "sickness," a "malady," and an "ailment," and alcoholics are characterized as persons who are "sick" or "ill." In the Personal Stories section of the third edition of the Big Book, one of the subtitles is "How Forty-Three Alcoholics Recovered From Their Malady."[44]

Kurtz (2002:5) states that despite the fact that "A.A. does not promote the disease concept of alcoholism," most members refer to their alcoholism as a disease. However, this can be regarded more as a metaphor than as a literal description in the sense in which the word disease is usually employed in technical medical terminology (Kurtz, 1979:199–202). Use of this metaphor removes the stigma generally attached to alcoholism in society, allowing A.A. participants to see themselves as "sick" rather than "bad" (Conrad and Schneider, 1980), and to assume the "sick role" (Parsons, 1952), so that recovery becomes possible. As will be shown in this chapter, dealing with and finally accepting this concept is crucial in enabling newcomers to move through the four progressive stages of becoming integrated into A.A.'s social world.

That being clarified, the second stage of the A.A. conversion career can be seen as a learning stage in which the newcomer begins to learn the A.A. ideology and technology, and the content of its belief system and program principles. Participation during this period may be either as a Tourist whose involvement is limited to what is required or necessary according to external pressures, potential rewards or consequences; or as a Regular who already is beginning to develop familiarity in relationships and a commitment to continuing participation. In either case, and despite the fact that participation precedes the actual conversion, the primary content of this stage reflects the Intellectual motif.

As stated, few newcomers to A.A. define themselves as alcoholics. The process of changing the definition of self involves both beliefs and feelings. One of the first things those who enter hear in A.A. is that alcoholism is a disease, and that they are not to blame for having it. But although it is a chronic and incurable disease, they can alter its course by following some simple guidelines.

It is not always easy, given the overall cultural attitudes toward alcoholics as deviants, for many to accept the disease concept. As it was put by a businessman in his forties returning to A.A. from a hospital following a relapse:

> It was hard to see that a disease was responsible for my drinking. I was always in control of everything in my life, and drinking should be no exception.

However, once this belief is established, since one is absolved from blame for disease (Parsons, 1952), it offers the possibility of a positive self-concept despite being alcoholic, and thus allows the newcomer to move closer toward accepting the alcoholic label. A woman interviewee, a counselor in her late forties with nineteen years of sobriety, told me: "When I came to A.A., I heard that alcoholism is a disease … well … if it really was a sickness, then I could accept it a lot better." And from a conversation with a young nurse in her twenties, sober four years:

> You'd think I would have known … being a nurse … Well that applied to my patients, but not to me. I was supposed to know better and control myself. So, being able to finally accept that disease concept freed me from fighting it so hard!

Another aspect of this second stage is beginning to learn the technology of A.A. Copies of the text of the Twelve Steps and Twelve Traditions are often hung on the walls of meeting rooms. Each meeting begins with a reading from Chapter 5 of the Big Book. Thus, even without effort, the newcomer is exposed to information on how to achieve recovery the A.A. way. A man of about thirty told me:

> At first I didn't understand what some of it meant … like my life being unmanageable … it didn't seem that way to me. But the more I heard

and talked to people about what was going on with me ... well, it started to make some sense.

And a woman in her forties talked about the effect of hearing the beginning of Chapter 5 in the Big Book read at A.A. meetings, in particular the lines which said "Rarely have we seen a person fail" to get sober in the program, with the exceptions being those who were simply "incapable of being honest with themselves" (AAWS, 1976:58).

> I heard that part of Chapter 5 read over and over. It said I had to be honest, and I think I realized for the first time that I never had been ... really.

These statements reflect a cognitive aspect to the conversion process that, despite the sequence of occurrence, is indicative of the Intellectual motif in that it occurs from receiving and processing information about alcoholism and the A.A. belief system. On the other hand, knowledge of the program is not usually sought without some social influence. Indeed, one of the things newcomers are constantly prodded to do by more experienced members is to "read the Book," meaning the book entitled *Alcoholics Anonymous* in which the basic principles of the program were first formulated in 1939, originally nicknamed "the Big Book" because the first printing of the first edition was done on very thick paper with fairly large type.[45]

Table 4 illustrates the aspects of the Intellectual motif that apply in the second stage of the A.A. conversion process.

Table 4

Stage II Conversion Motifs

	Intellectual
(1) Degree of Social Pressure	low or none
(2) Temporal Duration	medium
(3) Level of Affect or Emotion	medium
(4) Affective/Emotional Content	illumination
(5) Belief-Participation Sequence	belief → participation

It is important to note that there are few complete conversions that come about from this intellectual investigation or cognitive assessment alone. For instance, while the alcoholic label or diagnosis might be accepted—i.e., that one has a disease called alcoholism—the redefinition of self at the deeper phenomenological level as "being" alcoholic is not yet accomplished. In fact, some leave A.A. at this point, with the idea that knowing that they have a disease is enough motivation for them to remain abstinent and avoid a relapse; and often they return as recidivists, unable to do it alone. A young woman celebrating two years of sobriety said it this way:

> It took me six years to get two, because I was in and out so much! I kept thinking I could do it on my own; I knew I was alcoholic in my head, but I hadn't accepted it in my gut. I really got so tired of introducing myself at meetings as a newcomer. This time, I prayed to God not to make me go through that again. Well, so far I haven't had to say I'm a newcomer again for two years.

Nevertheless, out of desperation or fear of outside social consequences, or because they feel some degree of comfort in the social context, many continue to participate and to take on the role of the member.

Stage III—Taking the Role of the Member

One of the means by which people interpret meaning and define situations in order to determine action is through the process of "taking the role of the other" (Mead, 1934). Taking the role of the member means that newcomers act as members do. This process begins almost immediately on entering the social world of A.A., but may intensify once some level of commitment has been made to continue, for whatever reason.

This third stage of the A.A. career is likely to be the longest since it may begin on the first day and continue until one is fully integrated into the social world. It is also the most critical since it involves those processes that promote the assumption of values of the generalized other into one's own values and belief system. Thus when one begins this stage, participation may still be at the Stranger or Tourist level, but will soon become that of Regular, or even Insider, since those are among the member roles to be assumed.

The Experimental and the Affectional Motifs. Two conversion motifs are exemplified: these are the *Experimental* and the *Affectional.* The A.A. conversion is fostered by the *experience* of success in the role and/or the development of *affectional* ties to other members or to the group as a whole. In both these modes, belief follows participation in sequence and occurs over time, the primary difference being in the affective content which is, in the Experimental motif in the realm of thought, and in the Affectional motif, in the realm of feeling.

In the Experimental motif, the newcomer reflects a "show me" posture, and after conversion, experiences enlightenment. In the Affectional motif, one enters with a need for affiliation, and conversion brings a feeling of attachment.

Before describing these conversion experiences further however, it is appropriate to clarify some specific acts of membership. Although they generally occur in a somewhat ordered progression, they may also occur simultaneously. These acts are summarized in the instructions often given to newcomers by older members: "Go to meetings and don't drink between meetings; read the Book, get a sponsor and work the Steps."

Going to Meetings. The initial act of a member usually consists of attending meetings. The A.A. meeting provides the formal arena for fulfilling the basic purpose of A.A.—to "share our experience, strength and hope with one another" in order to help each other recover from alcoholism, as is stated in the Preface read at the beginning of A.A. meetings.[46]

By attending meetings, Strangers become Regulars in the social world of A.A. They become socialized, hearing portions of the literature read (including the Twelve Steps and Twelve Traditions) and they begin to learn the A.A. language. They hear that others have been where they are; they hear and see that these others are staying sober and that their lives are improving. They are told that this can happen for them too, if they follow their path.

Thune (1977) sees the life stories of members as the key to the process of developing the A.A. identity. In hearing these stories, the newcomer searches and finds himself or herself, and develops a sense of belonging which give credibility to the new definition of self as an alcoholic. Often, the person or persons whose life stories are closest to one's own become objects of identification, even affection. A young man in his early twenties told me: "I was struggling along with about two weeks sober when I first heard Jack D.... the things he said fit me all too well."

Finally, at meetings, newcomers are made to feel accepted on their own terms with encouragement, rather than pressure. From a fifty-year-old man with twelve years of sobriety:

At first, all I did was go to meetings. That's what the judge said I had to do. And I was there with a chip on my shoulder too! But no one lectured me. Everyone was friendly. So I started to listen.

Not Drinking Between Meetings. A.A. teaches that total abstinence is the only way to arrest the disease of alcoholism. However, it seems that the very nature of the disease works against the alcoholic's acceptance of that need for abstinence. The physical and psychological need for the alcohol have become too powerful, so that when the alcoholic contemplates abstinence as lifelong, it seems overwhelming and impossible One way in which the program assists the alcoholic with the compulsion to drink, is to focus on small, more manageable time-periods of abstinence. Hence the use of the slogan, "One Day at a Time."

Another aspect of this tactic is to encourage using meetings as time markings to help maintain abstinence. Thus the expression, "Don't drink between meetings." This is especially meaningful in the newcomer's early days when preceded with the recommendation that one attend a meeting every day. In the initial days of sobriety, these short-term goals are often all that the newcomer can handle. As a man in his late thirties told me during a conversation in the Alano Club:

> The first few meetings I went to, I was in a fog. I really didn't understand anything they were saying. I didn't want to drink anymore, but I didn't know how to stop. God knows, I had tried everything. Then a man ... I don't even remember who ... talked to me after the meeting. And he said I should try going to a meeting every day that week and just see if I could not drink between the meetings. Somehow that seemed like something I could do. And by the end of the week, I had seven days sober! It was like a miracle.

Reading the Book. Another act involved in taking the role of a member involves reading the A.A. literature. Newcomers are often given packets of pamphlets and sometimes even a free copy of *Alcoholics Anonymous*, the "Big Book." They are then encouraged to read some portion of the book each day. There are special A.A. meetings on the weekly schedule in most geographical areas for reading and studying two of the basic A.A. books. What are called Big Book Study meetings read through the text of *Alcoholics Anonymous*, while what are referred to as Step Study meetings read and discuss the book entitled *Twelve Steps and Twelve Traditions* (AAWS, 1953). The object of these meetings is to discuss how suggestions from these works can be applied to daily living. Members are also strongly encouraged to read from some sort of spiritually oriented meditation book every morning when they first get up. The one most often used is a little black book called *Twenty-Four Hours a Day*, written in 1948 by Richmond Walker, an early member of A.A. Above all, it is the reading of the literature that forms the foundation for learning the A.A. language, which is part of becoming a well-socialized member.

When A.A. members talk about their lives, their speech is filled with phrases and quotations drawn from this literature, especially the Big Book. One can observe them emphasizing in conversation that theirs is a "simple program," and warning of the dangers of overcomplicating it. They will tell newcomers that one of the first things they have to do is start becoming "honest with themselves." People telling their own stories before a group will frequently begin their talks by explaining the need to relate "what we used to be like, what happened, and what we are like now." They will often admit that their early failure to be successful in the program came about because they kept on seeking "the easier, softer way." And so on, with all of the quotable phrases above being drawn in these instances from a portion of the fifth chapter entitled "How It Works," which is frequently read at the opening of meetings:

> Rarely have we seen a person fail who has thoroughly followed our path. Those who do not recover are people who cannot or will not completely give themselves to this simple program, usually men and women who are constitutionally incapable of being honest with themselves. There are such unfortunates. They are not at fault; they seem to have been born that way. They are naturally incapable of grasping and developing a manner of living which demands rigorous honesty. Their chances are less than average. There are those, too, who suffer from

grave emotional and mental disorders, but many of them do recover if they have the capacity to be honest.

Our stories disclose in a general way what we used to be like, what happened, and what we are like now. If you have decided you want what we have and are willing to go to any length to get it—then you are ready to take certain steps.

At some of these we balked. We thought we could find an easier, softer way. But we could not. With all the earnestness at our command, we beg of you to be fearless and thorough from the very start. Some of us have tried to hold on to our old ideas and the result was nil until we let go absolutely.

Remember that we deal with alcohol—cunning, baffling, powerful! Without help it is too much for us. But there is One who has all power—that One is God. May you find Him now!

Half measures availed us nothing. We stood at the turning point. We asked His protection and care with complete abandon. (AAWS, 1976:58–59)

There are many references to the importance of reading the literature, not only in the instructions given by sponsors and the readings at the start of the meetings, but also in the testimonials of the members. An older woman in her sixties, with over twenty years of sobriety, talked about the emotional ups and downs experienced in the first few years of sobriety:

I went to a lot of meetings, and when I felt down and alone, I read the Book. It is no lie that there is an answer to every question in that Book! Sometimes I would pick up the *Twenty-Four Hour* book and just start reading from the beginning. I would keep reading until I started getting my sense of serenity back. It always worked!

Finally, members use expressions and phrases from the A.A. literature in everyday language. Examples of such usage can be heard whenever members are in conversation. One such conversation was heard in the Alano

Club lounge where a young man was telling another about how his attempts to take a short cut on a job-related matter had backfired. His friend responded: "That's what you get when you try to take 'an easier, softer way!'"

Getting a Sponsor. Another aspect of taking the role of the member involves getting a "sponsor." Sponsorship is a key normative feature in the A.A. experience, and it usually involves strong affectional ties. The newcomer selects a more experienced member to serve as teacher, guide, role model, and sometimes dispenser of "tough love" (York, York and Wachtel, 1985).[47] Especially in the early period of recovery sponsorship is an intense emotional relationship in which the newcomer is dependent on the sponsor for support, handholding, etc., during some painful emotional changes, but also for setting one straight should one stray from the path or seem to be sliding back. Often, sponsors are credited for much of the impetus toward conversion. From the young man previously cited, explaining his identification with the speaker, Jack D.:

> I knew I wanted him to be my sponsor. It was the smartest move I'd made in a long time. He was real tough on me ... but, if not for him, I wouldn't have made it.

The sponsor generally has considerable influence over the newcomer, who may be somewhat bewildered or emotionally unstable. It is recommended that sponsors be of the same sex to avoid the pitfalls of premature romantic attachments described in Chapter 2.

Working the Steps. Part of the sponsor's function is to guide the newcomer in "working the Steps." This process involves making a conscious effort to practice the principles spelled out in the Twelve Steps. For many, this means radical behavioral as well as attitudinal changes, such as admitting one's alcoholism, turning one's will over to a higher power, facing up to one's shortcomings, making amends to persons harmed and doing service or helping others. Taking the role of a member requires that the newcomer at the very least be making some effort to practice this program. Since these principles are considered the steps to a "spiritual awakening," necessary for a successful conversion, it is expected that those who do *not* live by them will remain in considerable emotional distress even if they go to meetings and are not drinking. A major milestone is achieved at Step Four, which involves making "a searching and fearless moral inventory of ourselves" (AAWS,1976:59). As a woman in her early fifties explained:

> It was the hardest and most painful thing I ever had to do. But once I had it all down on paper, being as honest as I could at the time, I felt different ... a sense of freedom to really start living my life.

Sharing Experience, Strength and Hope. Another act of the member is speaking at meetings. For some, this is done sooner than for others. However, in general, "sharing" at meetings becomes more of a member's act after certain milestones have been passed. For example, it was generally expected among the A.A. groups studied in this research, that whether one had already done so or not, one would be sharing at meetings after the thirty-day sobriety milestone, and no later than the ninety-day milestone.

The value of speaking at meetings is that as well as helping others, it forces one to reiterate the integration of the program into one's own life history, and thus reinforces before witnesses one's progress toward conversion to a new sense of self. As a long-time member in his sixties expressed it: "I love to speak at meetings. It's like making a Twelve-Step call on myself!"[48]

Doing Service/Helping Others. Finally, taking the role of the member usually means taking on the service responsibilities of an Insider. Service to others is an important tenet of the A.A. program, and reflects the fullest level of social world integration, since it involves creating the social world for others. It is embodied in the Twelfth Step, which endorses reaching out with the A.A. message, and is further reflected in the expression that once one has found success in A.A. one must "give it away in order to keep it." Service may involve Twelve-Step work through the central A.A. hotline or the Hospital and Institutions Committee or in agreeing to serve as a sponsor. It may involve leading a meeting, serving as meeting secretary, or making the coffee. It may involve service as a representative to the intergroup or working on the local newsletter. Doing service enhances one's credibility and fosters the bonds to the fellowship. A young man of about twenty-five, sitting in the Alano Club lounge, described his first experience on a Twelve-Step call:

> I was nervous when Mike asked me to go with him to see this guy. But after I got into it, it felt good. He went with us to the meeting. That was important to me, because I felt I was able to do what they say about carrying the message ... I really belonged to the fellowship now!

Perhaps the most powerful motivation for performing these acts is contained in the language of the Twelve Promises, a section from the Big Book which is often read aloud at meetings: (AAWS, 1976:83–84):

> If we are painstaking about this phase of our development, we will be amazed before we are half way through. We are going to know a new freedom and a new happiness. We will not regret the past nor wish to shut the door on it. We will comprehend the word serenity and we will know peace. No matter how far down the scale we have gone, we will see how our experience can benefit others. That feeling of uselessness and self-pity will disappear. We will lose interest in selfish things and gain interest in our fellows. Self-seeking will slip away. Our whole attitude and outlook upon life will change. Fear of people and of economic insecurity will leave us. We will intuitively know how to handle situations which used to baffle us. We will suddenly realize that God is doing for us what we could not do for ourselves.

> Are these extravagant promises? We think not. They are being fulfilled among us—sometimes quickly, sometimes slowly. They will always materialize if we work for them.

It is now possible to illustrate how performing these acts of membership leads to conversion in accord with the Experimental and Affectional motifs.

The Application of the Experimental Motif. As previously stated, most come to A.A. under some social pressure from outside. However, outsiders merely put pressure on alcoholics to comply with the program—to manifest the hallmarks of membership such as attending meetings and not getting into trouble because of drinking. They usually do not understand the true nature of success in A.A., which requires such intense identification. Furthermore, the pressure to convert from within is subtle and low-key. The individual is merely given guidelines to follow, and told that if he or she does so, the program will work. Once again, rather than being pressured toward a new self-definition, reluctant or doubting newcomers are simply told that if they "get the body to the meeting, the mind will follow."

From many of the stories of members, this is precisely what occurs. As the newcomer performs those core acts which accompany the role definition of a member, the benefits to health and social functioning which usually follow lead to genuine conviction that the A.A. way is the way to live. In many A.A. groups this is reinforced when the meeting is closed, when all the members say in unison, "Keep coming back; it works!"

Often the rewards of this behavior are so significant that even the most defiant become convinced. One example of this came from the testimony of a retired military man called Pete. He was in his forties and speaking on the occasion of his twelfth anniversary of sobriety. His remarks are paraphrased as follows:

> I am not one of those people who likes to be told what to do, and I came to this program kickin' and screamin' ... but I couldn't afford not to. Everything was on the line. So I bit my tongue sometimes ... no, not always ... hell, I'll always be a fighter that way, I guess. Still, I kept coming back. I read the Book, even though I argued with it a lot. And I didn't take that first drink one day at a time. Well, pretty soon, it started to sink in. My way never worked for me. But A.A.'s way was working. Man, if it could work for me, it could work for anybody, 'cause I was one hell of a tough nut to crack!

Again, this process of conversion is consistent with the temporal requirements of the Experimental motif, since the actual transformation of identity, behavior and worldview takes place over weeks, months, and even years. A construction worker in his late thirties and in his fourth year of sobriety commented:

> The first year I was sober, I was still not ready to say I was an alcoholic and mean it … I mean, I said the words, but deep down I still thought some day I could drink like other people … and it probably wasn't until my third year that I really felt O.K. about being what I was … an alcoholic.

The curiosity that, according to Lofland and Skonovd (1981) characterizes the affective content of the Experimental mode, is reflected in the initial stages of participation. Some newcomers may introduce themselves as someone who is trying to find out if they are alcoholic. Even many who state openly at a meeting that they are alcoholic may qualify it in a less formal context as a still-incomplete process for them. A thirty-five-year-old business manager recently discharged from a treatment program explained how he felt over coffee at the Alano Club:

> I just don't know. They said at the hospital I'm alcoholic. But … well, I guess I must be. But I don't know if I need this. I think if I have to, I can just stop drinking. Well, I'll go for a while anyway … maybe I'll find out.

Sometimes, as with those like Pete (whose remarks we quoted five paragraphs earlier), the "show me" posture is more one of defiance than curiosity. Nevertheless, although curiosity or defiance may characterize the affective content through the initial stages of the conversion process, once the person has become convinced, the emotional content seems to become one of illumination, as in the Intellectual motif, or of outright relief at finally having some explanation for "what is wrong with me."

Furthermore, once converted, A.A. members talk of experiencing a kind of calm which they refer to as "serenity." This concept of serenity, or what might also be described as an evenness of emotional reaction to the world, appears frequently in the A.A. literature and language. It can also be compared with what Antonovsky (1980) refers to as a "sense of coherence," a feeling that everything will turn out as it should. Antonovsky postulates that the greater the "sense of coherence, the less the stress, and the less the stress, the less the 'dis-ease.'" Thus, serenity is seen as a key to maintaining sobriety. The Serenity Prayer written by the noted American theologian Reinhold Niebuhr is utilized as a program tool.[49] A woman in her sixties with over fifteen years of sobriety told me:

> Nothing is more important than my serenity. I have learned in A.A. that there are "no big deals" and as long as I do what I'm supposed to, my higher power will take care of me. But if I lost that serenity, I'm vulnerable … and it could kill me.

Nevertheless, it should be noted that the quest for serenity might go on for many years after conversion has been achieved. A fifty-year-old man with twelve years of sobriety explained:

> I still don't feel that A.A. has all the answers for me. I know I am addicted to alcohol, and I can't drink. I'm no longer even afraid I will. But I haven't gotten that peaceful serenity yet.

Finally, with regard to the Experimental motif, Lofland and Skonovd point out that it is not unique to religious conversion, and may even be seen in terms of the concept of situational adjustment (Becker, 1964, cited in Lofland and Skonovd, 1981:379), with commitment being the end result of increasing adaptation. The additional factor involved in religious conversion and the A.A. process is "intensive interaction" (Lofland and Skonovd, 1981). In A.A., this is repeatedly emphasized in both meeting testimonials and in interviews. This, of course, supports the importance of the peer group as a key factor in A.A. success. But we can now see that its positive value lies not merely in support, but also in a more proactive encouragement and reinforcement for the redefinition of self which is necessary for personal success. The same woman previously cited on the occasion of her second A.A. birthday, told how the group played an important role in pushing her into finally being able to acknowledge her alcoholism, not only in her head, but also "in my gut."

> Whenever I was slacking off, hiding in my room, thank God for my
> A.A. friends who came and got me out and brought me here. They
> knew, even if I didn't yet, that this was where I belonged.

To be sure, there are instances where things may even get worse before they get better: families and jobs may still be lost, there may be financial setbacks, and in some cases, one must even do jail time. But often, if strong affectional ties have been formed, they will keep the newcomer coming back and giving some effort to performing in the role of member.

The Application of the Affectional Motif. The second motif exemplified in this career stage where the alcoholic takes the role of the member, is the Affectional motif. In keeping with this mode, it is important to note that "love" is a primary theme in A.A.—love in the sense of *agape*, rather than *eros*. It is allegedly "felt in the very rooms" where meetings are held. A.A. members speak of "loving" one another, although they may not "like" each other. Members may be seen hugging each other (of both opposite and same sex) before and after meetings and during anniversary presentations.

In addition, although the level of affective arousal is not extreme in the A.A. conversion, many members express their conversion experience as highly influenced by the "unconditional love" they felt given to them by other members, even when they themselves felt unworthy. A somewhat typical example is from the testimony of a young woman in her twenties with a little over a year of sobriety:

> I didn't want to be here. But I didn't feel I belonged anywhere. My par-
> ents had had it; my friends didn't exist anymore … I was down on
> myself bad … I even failed at suicide. But all of you loved me when I
> couldn't love myself. So I kept coming back. And now all my friends
> are here; it's where I belong.

Table 5 illustrates the way in which the Experimental and the Affectional motifs apply to the conversion career in Stage III.

Table 5

Stage III Conversion Motifs

	<u>Experimental</u>	<u>Affectional</u>
(1) <u>Degree of Social Pressure</u>	low	medium
(2) <u>Temporal Duration</u>	long	long
(3) <u>Level of Affect or Emotion</u>	low	medium
(4) <u>Affective/Emotional Content</u>	curiosity	affection
(5) <u>Belief-Participation Sequence</u>	participation → belief	participation → belief

Combined Motifs. Finally, it should also be noted that, because the A.A. conversion takes place in a social world context that offers a wide range of interactional experiences, some descriptions reflect elements of a combination of motifs. This is shown in the comments of the twenty-eight-year-old man whose stereotype of the alcoholic was a skid-row vagrant:

> I had a hard time accepting the alcoholic identity. I started going to meetings because my friend suggested it. She went and it worked for her. But I couldn't allow myself to think I was anything so terrible as an alcoholic. Then after going to some meetings, I learned that alcoholism was a disease. What that meant was that I could be an alcoholic and

learn to resolve problems in healthy ways ... and I can do that as long
as I don't take a drink.

In summary, what occurs in the process of taking on a member's role is
a gradual acceptance of the alcoholic identity and a bonding with the A.A.
fellowship. The group acceptance, support and encouragement without
pressure, the emotional rewards embodied in the meeting rituals, the
expressions of love, the exposure to role models with whom one can identify and form affectional ties, and the inspirational style of the A.A. language all combine to reinforce the newcomer's progress toward acceptance
of the new self definition.

Stage IV—Reaching the Moment of Truth
(Redefining Oneself as Alcoholic)

Here, I am speaking of the final stage of conversion, the actual moment at
which a member's conversion is complete, when one accepts not only the
label, but also the essence of being alcoholic. There is reference in A.A. to
one's "moment of truth," in which one grasps, at the deepest level of being,
the fact of one's alcoholism. The distinction is often made here between
the admission that one is alcoholic and being in compliance with recovery
versus the acceptance of one's alcoholic being and surrendering fully to
that recovery (Tiebout, 1959). Some A.A. members express this sense of
having the final acceptance of their alcoholism brought to them in a sudden moment by a force outside themselves they cannot explain. From a
woman in her early thirties: "I'm not sure what it was that told me ... I just
knew it ... suddenly I knew that this was who I was, and it was O.K."

Not all members are aware of having such a moment, but for those who
do, the primary feature of the experience is its brevity. In the Lofland and
Skonovd typology (1981), both the Mystical and the Revivalist conversion
modes involve a brief moment of radical reorganization, and their relevance to this final stage of the A.A. conversion should be examined.

Application of the Mystical Motif. Although the Mystical mode,
according to formulation, is one in which conversion precedes participation

and occurs in isolation, without social interaction, this aspect of A.A. conversion which involves the actual acceptance of oneself as alcoholic is qualitatively reflective of the intensity, depth and feeling of a moment of radical change in one's perception and worldview that characterizes this conversion motif. It is also true that many such moments in the A.A. conversion are experienced when the member is alone, apart from other human contact. However, it must be pointed out that even this apparently brief conversion experience occurs mainly *after* exposure to the A.A. precepts and life stories of other members, and after participation in the program activities; what is perceived as a mystical conversion may be more appropriately called a completed A.A. socialization.[50]

Furthermore, the quasi-religious content and style of the A.A. language, such as references to reliance on and communication with a "higher power" or "God, as we understand Him," promote the notion of a mystical experience; and descriptions of the experience are often expressed in terms of A.A. language. For example, from a man in his mid-fifties who claimed that he was never religious:

> It just suddenly occurred to me what a miracle it was for me to have been sober two months. I had never put two weeks together before. I just figured my "higher power" had something for me to do, so I had better accept who I was and let Him take charge. After all, He got me this far!

Finally, while there is sometimes a noticeable degree of affective arousal among A.A. members, and there is sometimes a feeling of awe, it must also be noted that *fear* is rarely, if ever, described. Rather, the primary affect involved is most apt to be one of relief.

It is as though the alcoholic had been searching frantically for an identity, and even the alcoholic identity is better than none at all—or better than an identity that implied something even more negative than that. From a woman of about fifty:

I really thought I was going crazy. Then to finally understand that it was due to the drinking ... that I was alcoholic. Just to have a name for it was a tremendous relief!

Thus, the Mystical motif, if modified, has a relevant application to this stage of the conversion, as shown by Table 6.

Table 6

Stage IV Conversion Motifs

	Mystical
(1) Degree of Social Pressure	none to little
(2) Temporal Duration	short (appears so)
(3) Level of Affect or Emotion	high (moderately)
(4) Affective/Emotional Content	awe, love, fear
(5) Belief-Participation Sequence	belief → participation

The Revivalist Motif not relevant. The other conversion motif that involves an experience of very short duration is the Revivalist. Although in this mode, belief follows participation, the moment of conversion is always in a social context. While many A.A. conversions also take place in a social context, it is not one that involves the extreme social pressure or frenzied quality associated with this type of conversion.[51]

It is also true that A.A. meetings are often filled with an uplifting quality. But the conversion experience described is again one of a calm rather than an exciting vein, and the actual reaching of one's moment of truth is as likely to occur when one is alone as it is in a social situation. A thirty-eight-year-old woman with multiple medical problems from her drinking told me:

> I had been praying every night when I went to bed and in the morning, reading the *Twenty-Four Hour* book. One night, it just seemed to be there when I was praying. I said, "God, I'm an alcoholic, and I can't drink or I'll die. But I'm turning my life over to You, and I'll do whatever You want me to do just to stay sober a day at a time." After that, the obsession to drink just seemed not to be there anymore.

Furthermore, despite the fact that life is experienced as better once the new definition and way of life are accepted, unlike Taylor's (1978) description of the aftermath of the Revival type conversion, there are letdowns.[52] As one long-time member put it: "In retrospect, the alcohol part is the easiest. It's life that's hard!"

Thus, the Revivalist motif has no real application in the A.A. conversion career.

Summary of Conversion Stages

To summarize, then, five of the six conversion motifs outlined by Lofland and Skonovd (1981) have some application to the A.A. conversion in one or more of the four stages delineated. The conversion experiences in the Intellectual and Experimental motifs are primarily cognitive ones while those in the Coercive, Affectional and Mystical motifs are mainly affective or emotional.

Table 7 summarizes the motifs that apply in each stage of the A.A. conversion career.

Table 7

Conversion Career Stages and Applicable Motifs

	Stage I	Stage II	Stage III	Stage IV
Intellectual	X	X		
Mystical				X
Experimental			X	
Affectional	X		X	
Revivalist				
Coercive	X			

Once the stages of the conversion process have been completed, the A.A. career continues, but with the self now redefined as alcoholic.

The New Alcoholic Self

The new definition of self as alcoholic leads the member to interact differently with others. A.A. provides a new and positive definition of the alcoholic in recovery, and the interaction with others whose life experiences and self-definitions are similar provides a sense of belonging not to be obtained in the larger "drinking society" where the deviant alcoholic role has led to anomie and despair.

But even with the conversion complete, the alcoholic generally remains attached at some level of involvement to the social world of A.A. There are basically two reasons for this. One is, as some previous examples given have suggested, that the A.A. fellowship has become a primary social group. The second is that in the context of the larger society's emphasis on alcohol, there is the belief on the part of these members that they must stay attached to stay sober and survive.

Conversion and Recidivism. In Chapter 2, it was suggested that recidivism could be due in part to a lack of full-fledged integration into certain aspects of the social world of A.A. It may also be seen as a result of incomplete conversion. In other words, the redefinition of self as alcoholic in one's essence is the culmination of the conversion process, and just as it is important to successful recovery, the lack of its accomplishment provides one explanation for failure and recidivism. While those who return to drinking may have accepted a *diagnosis* or *label* of alcoholism, they may not have really accepted the essence of their alcoholic being at a deeper existential level. This acceptance again presupposes that they can never *not* be alcoholic. Thus, the recidivism may be seen as due to an incomplete conversion. As a man in his mid-thirties with six years of sobriety talked about his previous return to drinking after ten months of sobriety: "I wasn't ready to accept it, I guess. I went to a lot of meetings. But I just didn't think I was like all those other people."

Summary and Conclusion

In this Chapter, I have explored the central theme of A.A., that successful recovery lies in the fact that one does not merely admit to having the "disease" of alcoholism, but comes to define oneself as being alcoholic in the very essence of self. This redefinition of self leads the A.A. member to an acceptance of the A.A. values, principles and way of life, and provides a sense of coherence referred to as "serenity," which allows him or her to live without drinking. I have demonstrated how this process of redefinition of self occurs by examining it within a framework of religious conversion types.

Using Lofland and Skonovd's typology of six conversion motifs, I have explained how five of these are reflected in the four stages of the conversion careers of many who enter the social world of A.A., although it must be acknowledged that there are sometimes variations in the patterns of successful A.A. conversions.

Some motifs, such as the Coercive, have limited impact that applies only on entry into that world, but not in later stages of the process, since the interaction situation does not promote this style of conversion. The Intellectual and Affectional motifs also have implication for entry into the social world, since some do enter after reading the literature or being given information about alcoholism, and others may enter because of affectional ties to other members who have been successful in the program.

The Intellectual motif also has application in developing the belief in the disease concept of alcoholism, which appears to be an important first step toward being able to accept the self-redefinition, since it allows the self-concept to develop in a positive way. But the A.A. conversion appears to take place over a period of time, longer for some than others, and develops from the social experiences and affectional ties formed in the process of the newcomer's gradually taking on the role of the full member. Taking the role of the member involves several acts, but especially certain core activities such as attending meetings, reading the literature, getting a sponsor, working the Steps, sharing at meetings and doing A.A. service work.

The predominant motifs revealed in the A.A. conversion are the Experimental and the Affectional, in which taking the role of the member leads to affectional ties with members and/or improvements in health and social functioning, and in receiving social and emotional rewards. A notable variation on the Experimental motif is that while the affective content throughout the process may be one of curiosity, at the moment of actual acceptance, it appears to be one of either illumination or relief, with a post-conversion feeling of serenity.

The affectional ties formed to other members or to the group as a whole are reinforced by the experience of feeling love and acceptance from others, from identifying with their life stories, and from forming an attachment to a sponsor who serves as a program guide and role model.

Because of the wide range of social interaction experiences available in the social world of A.A., some conversion experiences reflect a combination of Intellectual, Experimental and Affectional elements. Furthermore, in the moment when the new definition of self becomes solidified, the experience often described is one that is qualitatively similar to that in the Mystical conversion. However, it is important to recognize that, unlike a true mystical conversion, most often this has been preceded and influenced by considerable exposure to the program and the A.A. language, and to social interaction with members.

Although A.A. meetings are often uplifting, they do not reflect the frenzy or high degree of social pressure to convert which is observed in the Revivalist mode of religious conversion. Also, the A.A. member's moment of truth is just as likely to occur when he or she is alone as it is in the presence of others. Thus, the Revivalist mode has least application to the A.A. conversion experience.

In general, A.A. conversions tend to differ in whether or not they are primarily dependent on cognitive or affective processes. But once conversion is complete, the new alcoholic self fully adapts to the A.A. way of life, which the member believes must be totally adhered to, in order to prevent relapse and recidivism.

5

A Typology of A.A. Members

The previous chapters suggest that successful A.A. membership requires the integration of the alcoholic into the A.A. social world to the extent that he or she experiences the interactions that lead one to the A.A. conversion—i.e., the acceptance of the alcoholic self identity and the development of the values, beliefs and behaviors which support recovery from alcoholism; further, that some degree of ongoing involvement in A.A. is seen as necessary to sustain that recovery. This integration is generally accomplished by the newcomer taking the role of the member, attending meetings, reading the literature, practicing the principles with the help of a sponsor, doing A.A. service work, and participating in some informal A.A. social life. The same activities, perhaps to a lesser extent, comprise a member's ongoing involvement.

The data also suggest that there are variations among A.A. members in the pathways to their integration and in the experiences of their conversion careers. From these variations, a member typology may be established. Earlier efforts to establish a typology of A.A. members include Rudy (1986), who established one based on whether the alcoholic self-identity was accepted before A.A. participation (Pure Alcoholics) or after (Convinced or Converted Alcoholics), and on the extent to which drinking experiences were important in testimonials (Convinced Alcoholics). Denzin (1987) established a typology of Recovering Identities, Transitory vs. Enduring (or Uncommitted vs. Committed). These may be seen as basically related to the levels of integration into the social world—i.e., Transitory or Uncommitted types are Strangers and Tourists, while Enduring or Committed types are Regulars and Insiders.

However, neither of these typologies relates the experiences of the members directly to their A.A. conversion. Furthermore, despite the appearance that some members have come to A.A. already convinced of their alcohol problem and need for help, the successful conversion to belief in one's alcoholism at the phenomenological level inherent in the A.A definition, is rarely if ever achieved prior to A.A. participation and full-fledged integration into the social world.

In this chapter, I will define two broad types of successful A.A. members that appear to be predominant in the A.A. social world. These types will be referred to as Sociables and Individualists, and descriptions of them will be informed by characteristics elaborated in previous chapters, including:

1) A high or low degree of self-concepts and behaviors associated with affiliative need or group dependency.

2) Individual versus group focus of A.A. participation.

3) Cognitive versus affective content of the conversion experience.

These types will also differ from Rudy or Denzin's types in that they do not describe types of alcoholics, but rather types of social world participants.

Analytical Framework

The operationalization of low or high group dependency and affiliative need will be based largely on self-perceptions of those interviewed and on the primary focus of their social interactions within the social world. Those who described themselves as "people oriented," with a predominantly group focus in their social interactions and behaviors, are viewed as having a high level of group dependency and affiliative need; while those who described themselves as "loners," with a predominantly individual focus in their social interactions and behaviors, are viewed as having a low level of group dependency and affiliative need.

Specific indicators of group-focused characteristics and behaviors include comfort in the A.A. group setting, friendliness, sociability, affectionate gestures, willingness and even eagerness to "share" at meetings, and the personal nature of the information shared. Service activities that may be associated with these characteristics include, but are not limited to, speaking at and leading meetings, serving on committees that reach out to others in groups, and organizing or participating in A.A. social events such as dances, picnics, etc.

Indicators of individual-focused characteristics and behaviors include physical detachment from the larger group, involvement in ongoing dyadic or small group rather than less personalized and transitory large group interactions, reluctance to "share" in the group setting, and a more general or impersonal nature of the information shared. Service activities may be limited to support type tasks such as making coffee, setting up the meeting or activity room, cleanup, limited sponsorship or Twelve-Step work, and behind-the-scenes organizational activity.

Levels of participation in the social world are defined according to the Unruh typology of Stranger, Tourist, Regular and Insider, the dimensions of which are delineated in Chapter 2. Strangers and Tourists represent a low level of participation while Regulars and Insiders have a moderate to high level of participation. The Stranger may have an awareness of the social world, but no deep knowledge of it or identification with it, and relationships are unfamiliar. The primary factors in the Tourist type are irregular participation, involvement for reward or lack of negative consequence, absence of commitment to the social world and termination of participation when the reward is no longer forthcoming. The Regular has commitment to the social world and is involved in its continuance. Relationships are familiar, but he or she does not create the social world for others. This is the role of the Insider, the A.A. member involved in the various forms of service work.

Finally, the Lofland and Skonovd typology of conversion described in Chapter 4 will be the basis for the dimension involving the experiences leading to the transformation of self-concept and acceptance at the deepest level of one's alcoholic being. As demonstrated in Chapter 3, the majority of A.A. conversion experiences are within the Experimental and Affectional motifs. In both of these modes, belief follows participation, the duration of the conversion is fairly long and the end result is the feeling of serenity. But experiences of the Experimental motif fall into a cognitive or learning arena, wherein social pressure and affect are low and the content of the affect is illumination or awareness. Those of the Affectional motif fall into an affective arena, wherein social pressure and emotion are moderate to high and the content is one of emotional attachment. Thus, A.A. members will be described as having a primarily cognitive or affective conversion.

Type Contrasts

While many members may have characteristics of both types—that is, there may be variations on each theme—the following descriptions delineate contrasts that generally apply.

Sociables. These members may enter the A.A. social world in any of the ways described in Chapter 4, due to pressure from family, friends, health professionals or agents of social control, or to maintain or foster pre-existing affectional ties with a current member. The notable feature of their entry is that by and large, they seem to have a feeling of almost immediate social comfort in the group setting, and it is this feeling which keeps them coming back and enhances their participation. That is, they quickly advance from Stranger or Tourist levels of involvement to Regulars and even Insiders.

Besides attending meetings and finding sponsors, they also read the literature and work the Steps. But the primary sustenance and support for their sobriety comes from the interaction with and emotional ties to other people, and usually to the group or fellowship as a whole. Once again, the comment of the A.A. woman friend quoted in Chapter 2 illustrates this: "I knew I belonged the first time I went to a meeting. I felt the people there knew how to get what I wanted."

A man in his fifties with about a year of sobriety had a similarly positive reaction from the very beginning:

> I never expected to see people who were happy. I expected "down and
> out." But there were a lot of smiling faces ... and that really made an
> impression on me!

People of this type demonstrate a high level of group dependency and
affiliative need by being responsive to the attention and affection offered
by others. At meetings they are usually observed to be outgoing and
friendly, even physically affectionate toward other members, some of
whom may otherwise be strangers to them.[53] They share regularly at
meetings, where they may openly talk about feelings and personal problems, with little apparent concern about the fact that many in the room are
unknown to them. When upset or troubled, they actively seek out support
and assistance from other members. A woman of about forty spoke of her
reasons for joining the Alano Club: "I know there are always people here I
can talk to and share with ... even between meetings." And on her relationships with other members, she said:

> Many nights when I was upset and couldn't sleep ... especially in those
> first few months, I'd call them every day ... sometimes three and four
> in the morning ... every person in the program whose number I had!

In most instances, these members describe themselves as "people" people. Although some of them said they were "shy," or not necessarily "joiners" when it came to formal organizations, they nevertheless enjoyed being
around people in both large and small numbers. Again, as stated by a
woman cited in Chapter III: "I am a 'people' person ... I need people."
And from a man in his early thirties with two years of sobriety: "I may be
basically shy, but I love to be around people!"

Although from a cultural perspective, it might be expected that this
group would be largely female, there are men in A.A. who appear to fit this
type also. For example, a man in his late thirties shared at a meeting: "I can
talk about things here that I can't talk about anywhere else ... it's O.K. to
have feelings." Another man, in his fifties, with ten years of sobriety
stressed the importance for him of this part of the program:

I have always needed people. But until A.A., I was too afraid of rejection to risk reaching out. Most of all here ... I love getting all the hugs!

In the early stages of the A.A. career, Sociable types may have relapses or "slips" that seem related to competing social world allegiances. A woman executive just returning to A.A. after a slip, said while sharing at a meeting:

It wasn't that I didn't like it. I enjoyed the friendliness and the comfort. But it was hard to get to meetings when I was on a project ... working so many hours.

And from a man in his early thirties:

The people I met in A.A. were O.K., but I didn't see why I had to give up my buddies. I convinced myself that I could go into the bar and just have a coke ... and at first, it was no problem. But soon, I was there instead of being at a meeting!

Once the affiliation with A.A. has solidified however, "slips" may be more associated with a personal emotional crisis for which the supports developed are somehow not adequate or not utilized. The story told by a middle-aged widow, who was sober for ten years, but then returned to drinking following the death of her twenty-four-year old son in an auto accident, illustrates this kind of slip:

I isolated myself from everyone, even my closest A.A. friends. I couldn't go or call. Once or twice, someone called me. But after I kept making excuses and said I would be O.K. enough times, it stopped. I just couldn't seem to get off the pity pot ... and the next thing I know I was drinking again.

As Regulars and Insiders, Sociable types participate in a variety of activities and services within the A.A. social world, especially those that involve others and are essentially group focused. That is, they are often leaders of meetings, members of Hospital and Institutions committees, telephone volunteers and Twelve-Step workers. They tend to sponsor newcomers, sometimes several at a time, and are often active in an Alano club and in organizing A.A. social events, both formal and informal. Their interactions generally involve a wide circle of other members, and their relationships are of both a primary and secondary nature. Thus, while they may develop primary friendships and small group associations, they perceive the fellowship as a whole as an extended family, as exemplified by the Sociable young man cited in Chapter II who found A.A. conventions like "family reunions."

Sociable types, for the most part, have conversion experiences that are emotional in nature. That is, they are largely of the Affectional type described by Lofland and Skonovd (1981). They tend to use language that signifies emotion. As mentioned, they often speak of warmth from the group and feelings of love in the meeting rooms. A statement heard many times in testimonials emphasizes this: "I love everyone here, even though I may not like some of you."

Although conversions may occur over a period of some time, members often report a moment in which they received some "sign" of the presence in their lives of a "higher power." A woman in her sixties with several years of sobriety described a situation where she almost drank again at Christmas of her third year:

> Life had been the pits for me that year. I was feeling lonely, since my family was all scattered. A woman at work invited me to a party, and the booze was flowing. I figured I might try to have just one glass of punch. But something came over me just as I was about to pour it. I thought, "I'm an alcoholic … an alcoholic … and this could kill me!" I left the party and drove to an Alkathon. And all the way over, I kept saying, "thank you God."

It should be explained that an Alkathon is a sort of continuously running A.A. party, held during holiday periods like Thanksgiving, Christmas, and New Year's, which may go on for up to twenty-four hours or more, with meetings being held on the side, and lots of food and non-alcoholic beverages. People can walk in any time they want to, and attend a meeting, or sit and chat, or play cards, or sometimes watch a football game on television. The A.A. groups in a community put these Alkathons on because they are aware alcoholics may be more vulnerable to destabilizing emotions or other pressures that may lead to a relapse during these holiday periods.

Interviewees of this type also reported some of the more rapid conversions without subsequent doubt. A man in his forties, who was observed to be very gregarious and affectionate with others, stated categorically: "Once I made the connection, there was never any doubt for me that I was a 'real' alcoholic."

Individualists. Before coming to A.A., both Sociables and Individualists may have reached what is referred to as a "low bottom" in which they have lost many or all social supports and experienced intense "negative labeling" (Trice & Roman, 1970a) in the larger society, perhaps having had serious illnesses from drinking and/or confrontations with the legal and criminal justice systems. However, of these two types, it is the Individualists who are more likely to fit the old traditional stereotype of the down and out alcoholic—mostly male, self-absorbed, socially isolated "loners" whose drinking often leads to hitting an extremely low bottom, where they may even end up on "skid row." We can hear this type speaking in the following words spoken in the Alano Club by an unemployed man in his early forties who was living in a recovery home and had less than a year of sobriety:

> I had sunk just about as far as I could. No job, no family, no real home. I'd been in jail and in "detox" … and in the V.A. [Veteran's Administration] hospital. A.A. is really my last hope!

Even those of this type who do not reach such "low bottoms" and may even seek other kinds of treatment on their own, seem to enter A.A. reluctantly, usually out of fear or after being ordered or pressured by a treatment program, an employer, judge, or other agent of social control. This is reflected in the statement of a fortyish man:

Even after I thought I might have a problem with booze, I was determined to lick it myself. I certainly didn't think of it as a disease ... and that I needed help ... and you wouldn't catch me dead going to one of those meetings! It took almost losing my job to get me here.

And from a fiftyish woman:

I knew I had to do something, I called my doctor, thinking he would put me in the hospital. But when he suggested A.A., I just couldn't see myself talking about my problems to a bunch of drunks! Thank God, I came anyway, 'cause I was scared I'd die!

Essentially people of this type correspond to the non-affiliators described in Chapter 3. They are initially uncomfortable around strangers and in the sometimes large, impersonal group setting of the A.A. meeting. A woman in her thirties, sober ten years, made a statement typical of this type:

At first, I was shy, even scared. There was so much noise and laughing ... I didn't understand how they could be laughing.[54]

A man in his late forties with six years sobriety indicated how the discomfort with large groups of people can continue among those of this type:

To this day, I like a small meeting. I mean I can handle the bigger ones, but I rarely talk there ... I'm just not as comfortable.

Naturally enough, the Individualist types, because of their feelings of discomfort around groups of people, may remain Strangers or Tourists for longer periods of time than the Sociable types, and be more likely to leave the social world without having advanced to Regular or Insider status. One man in his fifties had been in and out of A.A. five times over a period of twelve years, never having achieved more than four months of continuous sobriety. On this occasion, he had just received his one-year birthday cake. As he explained:

> I would go for the thirty days or the ninety … whatever the judge ordered … I didn't like it at all. But I saw it as "doing my time."

As non-affiliators, the Individualist types described themselves as preferring solitary or one-to-one activities. For example, a man in his forties, with about five years sober, said:

> I have always been a loner … very few friends. When I do anything, it's maybe with one other person I know pretty well.

As reflected in Chapter 3, the participation of these persons in the A.A. social world is slow to develop. At first they may do little else but attend meetings, if not to meet requirements, then because despite their discomfort in the group setting, they find a sense of security there. A businessman in his fifties with ten years of sobriety, when describing his early days in the program, said: "I went to meetings every day because I was safe there. As long as I stayed off the streets, I wouldn't drink."

However, since higher levels of social world integration appear to be required for A.A. success, Individualists who are successful must also become social world Regulars and Insiders.

In contrast to the Sociables whose involvement is fostered by their comfort in the supportive group setting, Individualists usually become involved through a process described more fully in Chapter 3, which begins with the formation of a significant one-to-one relationship. As illustrated, some Individualists do develop a degree of comfort with group activity. But most continue throughout their A.A. careers with social interactions limited to a few close associates. They share sporadically and often reluctantly at meetings. If affectionate at all, they are only this way with a few chosen individuals they have come to know quite well.

Often the dyadic relationships formed by these types expand into small cliques. An example of this is what I will call the "breakfast club." At the

Alano Club where I was an associate member and carried out much of my research, there was a small group of older men who had been in the program for many years and who met regularly for breakfast together there, but were rarely, if ever, around during the evening or peak hours of social activity.

Again, the Insider service work of Individualists tends to be focused on activities that do not require a high level of social interaction. While Individualists may engage in Twelve-Step work and in sponsorship, they are not always comfortable with these roles, and may do them sporadically or with more limitations or selectiveness, and with mixed success. As a sixty-year-old man with thirteen years of sobriety told me: "I just don't feel I have the ability to deal with someone else's emotions."

On the other hand, a forty-two-year-old woman who had forced herself to be a sponsor of three newcomers over a course of about ten years said: "It was very difficult, but in a way, I think doing it saved me!"

Other activities of this member type may involve meeting support tasks such as setting up the room, making the coffee, maintaining the literature, and behind-the-scenes organizational work. For example, some members of the same Alano Club who, like the men in the "breakfast club," were not into the more social aspects of the fellowship, were known to be among the planners, and in some cases financial supporters, of Twelve Step rehabilitation houses and Alano clubs. These Insiders were sometimes specifically consulted about operational problems of the Club. For example, during the first few years of my Club association I would often hear people talk of "asking Harry" about certain issues. But I never saw Harry until I went to the Club on a weekday for breakfast. He was one of the Club's founders, an elderly, white-haired gentleman who seemed somewhat aloof, except with a few other cronies with whom he interacted.

The conversion experiences of Individualists are largely cognitive. That is, they are based more on thought processes than on feeling ones, on gathering of information and observation of the interactions between changes in behavior and belief and changes in situation and condition. That is not to say that they are not affected at all by feeling for others. But the social pressure is relatively low except perhaps for that exerted by a sponsor, and they are more likely to be influenced by their own experience of progress than by emotional attachments or group pressure. For example, as it was explained by the young man in his thirties with three years of sobriety (the one who was cited in Chapter 3): "At first, I really didn't want to do what my sponsor was telling me I had to. But the more I did it, the better I felt."

These people generally have the "show me" posture of the Experimental conversion type described by Lofland and Skonovd (1981). Again, in this conversion motif, becoming abstinent from alcohol and acting the role of the member eventually lead to improved health and social functioning, which in turn lead to an illumination of a logical association between those activities and those results. For example, a fifty-one-year-old businessman who described himself as a loner said during an interview:

> There was no burning bush, no revelations. I just plodded along. In three months, I was back to work, my eyes got color, and I didn't gag every morning!

Table 8 illustrates the contrasts between the Sociable and the Individualist types.

Table 8

Contrasting Member Types

	Sociables	Individualists
Level of Group Dependency and Affiliative Need	high	low
Level of A.A. Participation	moderate to high (group-focused)	moderate to high (individual-focused)
Nature of A.A. Conversion	affective	cognitive

Mixed Types. As previously noted, in some cases, members who are primarily Individualists or Sociables have self-perceptions or experiences that fit those of the contrasting type. For instance, a few of those interviewed who were primarily Individualists and were not comfortable in the group, nevertheless had self-perceptions that were indicative of group dependency. One Individualist man told me: "I am not a group type person really. But I am affectionate … and I took to the caring behaviors." And another admitted: "I liked the hugging."

Some Individualists said they "wished" they could be more group oriented, and some eventually did develop a degree of comfort and group focus through participation in the social world, along the lines of the social construction process described in Chapter 3.

On the other hand, many Sociable types who were strongly influenced by the group acceptance and support, were also helped (just like the Individualists) by special dyadic relationships and the cognitive processing of messages in the literature and in testimonials, as well as by their own experiences. Therefore, both types had elements of their conversion experiences that reflected the contrasting type. But it will be left to further research to refine these variations and combinations, and perhaps to define additional types or subtypes.

Case Examples

Let us take a closer look at two Sociables, Joan and George, to see in more detail how these factors interact.

Joan B., a fifty-six-year-old secretary, had first come to A.A. when still in her twenties. In addition to alcohol, she had been hooked on street drugs, and this had landed her in prison. Thus, her A.A. career began in a Coercive mode: "I was ordered to go." However, this quickly shifted to an Affectional format, illustrating her high level of group dependency and affiliative need:

> At first I thought, "This is a good program for those alcoholics … but not me" because I thought an alcoholic was someone out of control …

in the street. That wasn't me. I had a drug problem. But then, I started getting social … I'm an extrovert … always a group type person. And I liked the people.

But on this first try, she did not progress past the Tourist level of involvement, and when she got out of prison a couple of years later, she took up with her former friends in the competing social world of drugs. As she told it:

> I really didn't think I was getting anything out of it. To me, even though I liked them, the people sounded too negative about their problems. I thought the people in the drug scene were more fun.

Back in prison a few years later, Joan returned to A.A., still a Tourist: "I went for the doughnuts!" But this time her emotional ties to the group grew stronger:

> These people were really "cool." When they talked, I heard them. If I missed a meeting, I really felt like I missed something. I asked a lot of questions because I still couldn't conceive of doing things without drinking or using.

Once out of prison, Joan continued to go to meetings and met more people. Although she struggled with her acceptance of her alcoholism, "I made a commitment to change my life." She became an A.A. Regular and found a sponsor. She began to participate as an Insider, serving on the Hospital and Institutions Committee. She remained sober for a year. Although she had a "slip" it was very brief, and she returned to the program almost right away. She explained it as follows:

> I realized that I had changed my values and "partying" was no longer the great thing. I had a sense of responsibility and I was better at self-discipline because of the things I had heard and seen in that year.

Joan's level of dependence on approval, support and interaction with others is illustrated in another less productive way. Despite the fact that she was able, in the context of the fellowship, to stop drinking and shooting heroin, she continued to take "pills." She attributed this in part to the "mixed messages" she was getting from other members.

> No one seemed to want to talk about that. Some people even said it didn't matter, as long as I didn't drink. So for a time, I rationalized that it was O.K.

Joan had another relapse back into drinking ten years later. This was related to emotional issues in her marriage and her husband's addiction, which culminated in his death a few years later. Although she stayed involved in the A.A. social world, her conversion was not to be complete until a few years after that, when she was influenced by other members to begin getting more into the spiritual aspects of the program. She describes this as an emotional experience:

> People kept telling me I had to work the Steps if I wanted to feel better. I began meditating. It gave me energy, and I started to feel my spirituality.

She gave up other drugs and sought additional help through professional counseling. Things also began to get better in her life. She married again, and began a career as a legal secretary, having gotten training in prison. Gradually, she developed a greater self-acceptance that she explained this way:

> I realized I only had myself. There was nothing to hide behind anymore. And it was O.K. to be me. I finally accepted myself.

However, Joan still attributed her success in A.A. in large measure to the support of others.

> The people have been the most important thing. When I was sick, they called ... sent flowers ... people came into my life through the fellowship and they have been like family. It took me many years to accept

myself and the spiritual part of the program. But the people kept me going.

At the time she was interviewed, Joan had been sober in A.A. for almost sixteen years. She had survived another divorce and a serious and painful illness, including several surgeries and a resultant loss of her career. Nevertheless, she had remained free from alcohol and other mind-altering drugs, although still smoking cigarettes. Besides her primary live-in relationship, she claimed a wide circle of A.A. friends, and continued to participate as an A.A. Insider, going to meetings, reaching out to newcomers, and sponsoring several women. She was involved with a non-profit alcoholism rehabilitation corporation, and had become the president of its board of directors.

George A., a thirty-six-year-old baker, two years sober, described himself as somewhat shy around strangers, but "a bar drinker ... a local neighborhood bar with people I grew up with. I always liked to be around people." His first introduction to A.A. was through an old drinking buddy he ran into at the bar. As he described it:

> He was drinking 7-UP. I asked him about it. He said he hadn't been drinking for quite a while and was going to meetings. It was like a revelation to me that someone could not drink and be enjoying the type of life I did.

Eventually, George's own drinking led to both physical and job problems. Although told by his doctor that he should "do something about it," he was not offered any specific direction. At work, he was disciplined and finally suspended. He described his reaction:

> I tried to quit drinking on my own, even substituted other drugs ... "hash," "crystal," ... but it didn't work because I started getting dependent on that ... and I ended up drinking again too!

At that point, since George had promised his mother that if he could not do it on his own, he would get help, he called A.A. In his words:

I said I think I need to go to a meeting. He said that it would be easy with over six hundred of them a week, and he sent me to my first. Some of my friends had gone to that same one!

George was immediately comfortable:

It was different for me. I announced myself as a newcomer and an alcoholic ... even I didn't expect that! I saw that some of these people seemed to be on top of things, despite their problems. And there were all types ... women and men, all ages. I felt good. There were suit and tie types, sporty types and types like me. I heard the message that it was possible to change my life, and I felt I could fit in A.A.

George became a Regular in both formal and informal aspects of the social world. He went to ninety meetings in ninety days and worked the first three Steps almost immediately. He recalled:

I remember telling God as I walked to my car after the first meeting that ninety meetings seemed like a lot to me. But if this is how it is supposed to be, I'd do my best.

At first, George divided his time between meetings and shooting pool at the bar with his old buddies. But as he went to more meetings, they soon became a "substitute" for the bar. He got a book within the first week and read a lot of A.A. literature. He began socializing after meetings with other members, and found a sponsor at one of the coffee klatches. George took on a variety of Insider tasks including making the coffee and being a meeting secretary.

George's conversion was fairly rapid and primarily of the Affectional type. His acceptance of the alcoholic identity and the A.A. way of life relied heavily on the emotional attachment he formed with the group from the very first meeting, and it was then that he said he began to read the literature and to experience improvement in his life. "I got hope from the stories and the appearance of other people. Helping others has helped me too."

At the time of his interview, George was attending nine or ten meetings a week and sponsoring several newcomers. He was involved in an active A.A. social life, as well as continuing to attend to his spiritual program: "I pray every day and as often as the need arises. I read and write too, and keep in close contact with my sponsor."

Individualists Henry and Rose

Henry B., a forty-year-old single construction worker, came to A.A. when he was in his mid-twenties. He described himself as having been "outgoing when young," but never a "joiner." In the last few years of his drinking, following his service in Viet Nam, he had serious physical withdrawal, and became extremely ill. He described the results: "For about six months, I couldn't work, and then in the last few weeks, I could not even eat!"

He sought medical help, but explained: "The doctor didn't know what to do with me. His receptionist was in A.A. and she introduced me to Frank at the Alano Club. He took me to detox." After detox, Henry stopped drinking and continued to hang around the Alano Club because, as he saw it, "I had no place else to go."

It was suggested that he go to the Veteran's Administration hospital, and he entered the outpatient program there. The psychologist diagnosed him as being depressed, and he was admitted to the hospital, where he remained for six months. After he was released from the hospital, Henry worked in a sheltered workshop. He got an apartment near the Alano Club, and continued to hang around there. But he was still depressed, and did not yet accept his alcoholism. He expressed discomfort and added: "I only went to a meeting once in a while. I did get a sponsor, and we talked … but he didn't push me."

This peripheral involvement lasted two years. According to Henry, "It was fear that kept me sober." But hanging around the periphery did appear to have an impact on him.

> I started looking at those who were working the program, and those who were sitting around unhappy. It was clear whose lives were coming together.

Henry then increased his meeting attendance to three or four meetings a week. He began to work the Steps with the help of his sponsor, and through their relationship was introduced to other members. He became willing to try to share more at meetings and become more responsive to others. But his recovery was complicated by his depression, which he was trying to handle just by taking the medication prescribed for him. He was not doing anything to deal with the other parts of the Post Traumatic Stress Disorder from which he was continuing to suffer as a result of his experiences in Viet Nam. As he described it:

> I was sober, but not getting to feel any better. Finally, someone said, "You don't have to feel this way," and suggested outside help.

Henry saw a psychiatrist who sent him for counseling at a veterans center. Once his head was clearer, he was able to deal with some past issues, especially his Viet Nam experiences. This enhanced his A.A. conversion, which was of the cognitive illuminative nature:

> When I could think it all through, it became clear, and I could accept my alcoholic self. When I have a problem, I ask myself, "What does the program tell me to do? What do the principles say about this?"

Although he did not return to drinking, Henry's integration into the A.A. social world has been slow. His level of involvement has remained at the status of Regular, although he has tried assuming some service responsibilities. As he explained: "I led a meeting and was a secretary for a while. I tried sponsoring a few people, but I had problems with that."

Sober for seventeen years, Henry still goes to the Alano Club, but "much less." He attends a couple of meetings a month and keeps in touch with his sponsor and a few other A.A. friends. Still somewhat of a loner, he nevertheless has found a way to make the program work for him by turning to a book rather than a person: "When I am baffled about something, I open the Twelve and Twelve." (AAWS, 1953; this is the standard A.A. book explaining the Steps and Traditions).

Rose M., a fifty-one-year-old married teacher with five years of sobriety described herself as a "loner," and added: "I was reclusive most of my life. I drank alone." She first sought help for drinking in her mid-forties from a psychiatrist who put her on tranquilizers and Antabuse.[55] But she quickly began to abuse the tranquilizers and to take sedatives as well. Realizing she was in trouble, she called the employee assistance counselor who sent her to a specialist. He helped her get off the tranquilizers and recommended an A.A. meeting specifically for teachers. According to Rose:

> I did what I was told because I was very afraid. During the summer, I even went to ninety meetings in ninety days. But it was difficult, because I am not close to people. I forced myself.

During that first three months, she met a woman she was "attracted to," and who became her sponsor. During the first year, she became a Regular at the teachers' meeting, which was small and compatible. However, she told me, "Other than my sponsor, I was not close to anyone."

Nevertheless, she said, "I continued to go to meetings, and started to do some service work." She finally began to work the Steps and to meditate, and eventually became an Insider. She described her role as follows:

> I did lots of "gofer" work at first. But my sponsor encouraged me to lead some meetings too, and take a secretary's job. I couldn't do Twelve-Step work because my husband objected to the phone calls. But I did sponsor someone.

After the first year, Rose was able to be more comfortable than many Individualists with the more group-focused activities because she found a small group with whom she felt comfortable and simpatico: "I started to go to lunch with some other teachers on the program. Later, I started a new teachers' meeting." She found a level of comfort at the teachers' meeting that she had not expected. As she told it: "I found that I actually liked the warmth of the people coming up and hugging me."

Rose's conversion was basically completed in that first year, fairly rapid for an Individualist type. However, it was based largely on her experience of life getting better and her using the "tools" of the program, which she specified as "prayer, the Third and Fourth Steps."

At the time of the interview, Rose was still having some difficulty dealing with family problems, especially her husband's drinking. Through her A.A. experience she had become less reclusive and more comfortable sharing with others, but mainly was staying close to her core group. In her words: "There are some people I don't like, and some meetings I don't go to."

Summary and Conclusion

In this chapter, I have delineated two broad types of A.A. members: Sociables and Individualists. In general, Sociables have a high degree of group dependency and affiliative need. They perceive themselves as "people" people, and regardless of their means of entry into the A.A. social world, they often form an immediate emotional attachment, feeling comfortable in the group setting. Individualists, on the other hand, are not comfortable with strangers, describing themselves as "loners," and often remaining in the group environment of A.A. largely out of fear of social consequences and feelings of safety in being away from a drinking environment.

In the initial stages of participation, Sociables may leave while they are still only Strangers or Tourists, largely because of allegiances to competing social worlds, while Individualists are most likely to leave because of their discomfort with strangers and with the group environment. Because of their openness to group influence, Sociables may become integrated more quickly into the A.A. social world, while for Individualists, the process is generally slower, and tends to follow along the lines described in Chapter 3.

In addition, the way in which Regular and Insider roles are fulfilled may differ. For Sociables, participation includes one-to-one and both small and large group involvements. Their circle of A.A. associations is wide, including both primary and secondary relationships. For Individualists, these associations tend to occur largely in dyadic or small group relationships and are limited to a narrower circle of primary relationships.

As Insiders, Sociables take on a wide range of service work, including leadership of meetings and organizing social activities, while Individualists tend more toward behind-the-scenes services. Sociables may also have earlier spiritual experiences and more rapid conversions. Their conversions are largely of the affective type, while Individualists tend more toward cognitive ones. Nevertheless, many members have elements of both types in their self-perceptions and in the description of their activities and conversion experiences, so that additional research is needed to refine and define subtypes.

6

Conclusion

C. Wright Mills (1961) pointed out that many troubles that seem personal can best be understood and solved by viewing them in a larger context as social problems. This present work attempts to provide a new way of understanding the sociological component in individual recovery from alcoholism.

Alcoholics Anonymous is widely recognized as one of the most successful programs of long-term alcoholism recovery. However, unlike previous studies of A.A., which view it as a form of rehabilitation and focus on the personal aspects of recovery within its structure and program philosophy, or which merely postulate the importance of social factors such as group support, this study investigates A.A. as a social world. This different perspective allows us to examine certain social processes and interactions in a manner that gives a much fuller explanation of how and why A.A. works.

While Strauss' (1978) concept of social worlds suggests activity areas rather than organizations (e.g., the social world of tennis or of music), I have contended that A.A. can also be defined as a social world because it has given rise to a world of recovery activity that is larger than the initial voluntary association which spawned that world. The social world of A.A. now consists not only of the formal association, but of other organizations and associations, both formal and informal, within which social life is based on the A.A. principles and language of recovery.

A.A. encompasses a population that is worldwide, and its activity is not limited by specific time or space. Its program technology is communicated through face-to-face interactions in meetings and informal associations, and through its literature and symbols. Indeed, the term membership is misleading because association with A.A. occurs only through cognitive identification with the A.A. way of life, and not through being included on lists of names or formal membership rolls.

A.A.'s success has been attributed to several factors, among which are its accessibility, intense peer group support, the effects of re-labeling, and its program of spiritual growth. While each of these appears to contribute to that success, it is the transformation of self-identity and acceptance of one's alcoholic self at an existential level which seems to be the central factor in leading to the "sense of coherence" (Antonovsky, 1980) or "serenity" required for individual recovery. Religious conversion has long been viewed as a powerful prototype of such self-transformation, and A.A.'s philosophy has strong religious underpinnings. However, in the preceding chapters, the data presented illustrates for the first time how that conversion is brought about through social interaction processes, and demonstrates that success depends on social world integration.

The social world of A.A. functions as an extended family, providing a primary reference group which gives a sense of belonging and fosters a re-socialization process leading to the development of new basic values. The data in this work illustrates the precise nature of the group function, which is not support alone, but proactive in its prodding and pressure toward further integration and toward conversion itself. Yet the prodding is low key, not coercive. It is often administered as what is referred to as "tough love," or through the elitist language of the A.A. literature. But one can also see the strong effects of the group social acceptance, its affection, and positive kinds of group pressure.

Although most do not enter A.A. voluntarily, those that enter as Strangers, through exposure to its social world interactions and through taking the role of the member, may progress to higher levels of participation as Regulars and Insiders and eventually arrive at a completed conversion. In fact, so powerful is the impact of this social world, that it pulls in even some of the most doubtful and most unresponsive to group pressure or support. Furthermore, the social world provides the entire gamut of social interaction possibilities, including social activity, friendship, professional collegiality, love, marriage and even family togetherness.

Another area in which this research has provided a new understanding is in the uncovering of more than one type of A.A. member. It is often assumed by outsiders that there is a single pathway to A.A. success, and that members follow that path in similar cookie-cutter fashion. But as revealed here, there are variations in members' patterns of integration into the social world of A.A. and in their conversion experiences. Broad contrasts are drawn between those who appear to interact well with the group format of participation and those who are characterized as "loners," between those whose participation is largely group-focused and those whose participation is largely individual-focused, and between those for whom the content of the conversion experience is largely affective versus those for whom it is largely cognitive. These contrasts provide guidelines for perceiving at least two types of social world participants in A.A., which I have called Sociables and Individualists. The typology helps to understand not only how A.A. works for so many people, but suggests why it may not have worked for some of the others.

It is hoped that this study will aid students and researchers in social psychology and the sociology of health and illness by increasing their understanding of adult re-socialization and of the recovery process, and by raising questions for further research.

For clinicians and other health care professionals, the data has implications for policy and program development and offers a greater insight into how A.A works and how referrals to such change-enhancement programs can be made and utilized more effectively within a total treatment approach. Greater successes could be gained, for example, by giving different recommendations on program participation to the types this study calls Sociables and Individualists.

Notes

[1] Not including A.A. approved literature, there are listings of over one thousand books and pamphlets about A.A in each volume, many of which represent psychological, sociological and educational studies. In addition there are listings for several hundred scholarly journal articles, chapters about A.A. in books, and theses and dissertations on the subject.

[2] Leach and Norris' stages are as follows: (a) learning of the existence of A.A.; (b) perceiving A.A. as relevant to one's needs; (c) being referred to A.A. by a helping agency; (d) making first personal contact with A.A., perhaps by telephone or by letter, but more likely face to face, involving a visit to an A.A. office, clubhouse for A.A. members or being visited by an individual A.A. member or two, or attending an open A.A. meeting; (e) attending a "closed" A.A. meeting, i.e., for members only; (f) participating in various other A.A. activities, such as those related to the Twelve Steps and others which enable the alcoholic to internalize the norms of the movement, especially that of abstinence and those codified in the Twelve Traditions; (g) taking the last drink; (h) making a Twelve Step visit to help another alcoholic; and (i) speaking at an A.A. meeting, possibly resulting in disclosure to non-alcoholic acquaintances of one's A.A. membership. (Leach and Norris in Kissin and Begleiter, 1977:483–84).

Rudy's stages are (a) hitting bottom; (b) first stepping; (c) making a commitment; (d) accepting one's problem; (e) telling one's story; (f) doing Twelve-Step work (Rudy, 1986).

[3] In this model, *Pure* alcoholics are defined as those who believed they were alcoholic before coming to A.A., while *Convinced* alcoholics are those who are convinced of their alcoholism after attending A.A. and absorbing its ideology and information about how it relates to their behavior. *Converted* alcoholics are similar to Convinced alcoholics, but do not emphasize drinking in their accounts. Furthermore, their acceptance of an alcoholic identity is characterized by more organization pressure. Finally, *Tangential* alcoholics are characterized by a low emphasis on drinking and by a number of problem behaviors which may or may not involve drinking. (Rudy, 1986:62).

[4] A.A. is also described in its literature as a "program" of recovery, a "society" of men and women, a social "movement" and a "way of life."

[5] This will not include some groups which may appear to be A.A. connected, such as those foundations which maintain the homes of Bill W. (Stepping Stones) and Dr. Bob (Dr. Bob's House), as these are not A.A. facilities, but maintained as historic sites, and are open to the public.

[6] A.A. has conducted surveys of its own membership every three years since 1968. As acknowledged by A.A., fully accurate data are not really possible due to a number of problems, including the fact that not all those who consider themselves A.A. members attend meetings, belong to groups or complete the survey. However, A.A. states that it attempts to account for this in compiling its numbers. The latest reported numbers are 2,082,980 members, with 105,284 groups worldwide (AAWS, 2004).

[7] There are, of course, official statuses connected with those formal associations which make up the social world, e.g., Alano club members, conference delegates, General Service Office staff, rehab house residents, etc.

[8] To be more specific, in 1985, it was estimated at 18.3 million classified as heavier drinkers, with 12.1 million having one or more symptoms of alcoholism (NIAAA Dept. of Biometry and Epidemiology, 1985:5–6). In more recent documentation, the number of abusers varies from 13 million (Gordis, 1998) to 17.6 million (U.S. Dept. of HHS, 2000). In the latter documentation, the number of those seen as alcoholic is down to 7.9 million. However, it is pointed out that accurate data on the prevalence of dependency symptoms and the nature and magnitude of problem consequences of drinking are difficult to acquire, and that comparisons of large-scale national surveys are "hampered by differences in criteria for problem levels, in wording of survey questions, and in interpretation of data" (U.S. Dept. of HHS, 1987:12). Keeping in mind that alcoholism is considered in medical terms to be progressive and that the only requirement for A.A. membership is not alcoholism, but "a desire to stop drinking," the potential for affiliation with the social world remains quite large despite these variances.

[9] According to the 1989 A.A. membership survey (AAWS, 1990), 27% were self-motivated, while the rest were sent by others or "recruited" by an A.A. member. In the 2004 survey, 39% were referred by a health care provider (AAWS, 2004), probably reflecting the increase in available treatment and in the number of professionals more aware of the value of such referrals to their patients and of the increase in counselors who are themselves A.A. and/or N.A. members.

[10] Once again, this does not apply to the formal associations within the social world such as Alano clubs and rehabilitation houses.

[11] It may be that the imbalance of women and minority groups in A.A. partially reflects their status in society at large. Attention to women's alcohol problems increased in the 1960s and 1970s, with the rise of the new women's movement. It

was found that a marked increase in women drinkers was seen after WWII, and by the late 70s, it was estimated that from one-third to one-half of all alcoholics were women (Sandmaier, 1980). Accordingly, the female membership in A.A. increased from 22% in 1968 to 34% in 1986 and 35% in 1989 (AAWS, 1990). Current membership of women in A.A. reportedly remains at 35% (AAWS, 2004).

[12] The A.A. Traditions state that it shall be self-supporting through member contributions (AAWS, 1976:564). This includes money from meeting donations and literature sales.

[13] Because of my close association as a friend of the fellowship, I was privy to some informal customs not usually known to people outside of the A.A. social world. The choice not to reveal these expressions here was based on the fact that they are intentionally designed as codes, and would no longer be valid as such if their meaning were revealed to the general public. While it is true that other aspects of A.A. language revealed throughout this work might also be a "giveaway" if used in earshot of non members, these are not conditioned with the same intention and are largely based on A.A. literature, meaning that their association with A.A. is already available to the general public.

[14] The 1989 member survey showed this at 22%, an increase of only 1% from 1986, but of 15 to 20% between 1980 and 1983 (AAWS, 1990). The 2004 survey shows this at only 10%, possibly reflecting a lack of reporting on the part of Young People-specific groups, and/or a growth of other twelve step programs for drugs other than alcohol, which might be more relevant to the needs of this group.

[15] This went up from 18% in 1977 to 46% in 1989 (AAWS, 1990), which may also have reflected the increase in women during that same period, since A.A. women reported more other-drug use than A.A. men (AAWS, 1990). Interestingly, in the current survey, this is no longer an included category of information. As with the lower percentage of young people in A.A., this too may be due to the increased proliferation of programs appealing to those with problems with drugs other than alcohol, such as Narcotics Anonymous, Cocaine Anonymous, etc.

[16] There also developed considerable concern about people who came to A.A. meetings who were drug abusers, but claimed to have no problems at all with alcohol. An A.A. Archives Committee member told me that cofounder Bill W.'s 1958 article, "Problems Other Than Alcohol," is now an A.A. pamphlet.

[17] A so-called circuit speaker is one, usually with a significant number of years of sobriety, known as much for his or her speaking ability as for the quality of

recovery, who is invited to speak all over the country at numerous large A.A. conferences and state conventions on a fairly regular basis.

18 Alcoholics who are forced to live in almost complete isolation, such as lighthouse keepers or dwellers in isolated wilderness areas, who are unable to be members of a regular A.A. group, can register themselves with the New York General Service Office as "loners" and consider themselves A.A. members in that fashion. They are forced to maintain their involvement with the fellowship principally through personal correspondence and use of the media.

19 *Sober Times* ceased publication in the mid-1990s. The 2006 paper by Bishop provides full coverage of the history and nature of this controversy. A copy can be obtained from the author by writing to 46 Eureka Ave., Wheeling, WV 26003, or emailing bishopbk@comcast.net

20 The woman was a member of Al-Anon Family Groups, founded by Lois Wilson, wife of the A.A. founder. It addresses families and friends of alcoholics and shares the A.A. philosophy, purpose and technology. In the Al-Anon logo, the circle is placed inside the triangle, while in the A.A. logo, the triangle is inside the circle.

21 A group that met at the Alano Club I frequented, was a closed group for doctors and lawyers that was "doubly" concerned with anonymity, and so was called the Anonymous, Anonymous Group. However, other special population groups such as young people's groups were actually open for attendees of any age.

22 The passage read is usually a portion of Chapter 5 of the Big Book, "How it Works." (AAWS, 1976).

23 Needless to say, the southern California area which is the basis of this research, is not completely representative of A.A. in these matters of style. For instance, at a meeting I observed in my New York hometown, people did not form a circle or hold hands for the ending prayer. At a meeting I attended in Jerusalem, Israel (see note 27), the Serenity Prayer was used instead of the Lord's Prayer. Also the phrase "it works" was not heard until the late 1970s or later. It seems to have been tacked on by graduates of certain treatment facilities.

24 A term which has fallen into some disrepute. Treatment professionals prefer "relapse," and some A.A. members themselves see the use of the word "slip" as a handy way of avoiding responsibility for those not working their programs. Nevertheless, if one takes literally the notion of following a path to recovery, it seems a perfectly appropriate word to symbolize straying from that path.

25 I recently learned from a member of this group that meetings have been held annually since 1996. The meetings, held in a different city each year, offer workshops which draw A.A archivists and historians from all over the U.S. and Canada.

26 It is not uncommon for members to help each other find jobs, homes and services, and provide business for other members with particular skills. A man in his early forties with several years of sobriety and training as an auto mechanic, on retiring from the military, began working on cars of members he met through the Alano Club. Within a year, he had developed this into a small business with his customers coming almost exclusively from the fellowship.

27 On a trip to Israel in 1977, I located an English-speaking A.A. group in Jerusalem. Although a total stranger, as an A.A. associate, I was immediately welcome in a foreign country. The woman in whose home the closed meeting was held, telephoned all fourteen members of the group to take a "group conscience" vote which allowed me, as a non-member, to attend the meeting. Afterward, I was invited to private homes for dinner and treated as a family member because of my association with the fellowship.

28 The term "ninety-day wonder" was first used during WWII to describe those enlisted men who were made officers after three months of Officers Candidate School. According to a family member of mine, a "ninety-day wonder" who is now a retired U.S. Army Major, the term was used both positively by the new officers—i.e., "There was tremendous pressure to learn a lot very quickly. The fact that we made it through was truly a wonder!"—and negatively or sarcastically by others, especially those who went through more traditional officer training at military academies. A.A. usage of the term is of the latter negative variety.

29 In the early 1970s, I served on the local committee for counselor certification of a California-based organization called Counselors on Alcoholism, Addictions and Related Disorders (CAARD), which was founded by such A.A. members. It later disbanded and was replaced by a group still in existence as the California Association of Alcohol and Drug Administrators and Counselors (CAADAC). In addition, there is at least one such organization at the national level, the National Association of Alcohol and Drug Administrators and Counselors (NAADAC.) In the last few decades, there has also been an increase of recovering people who have become or are becoming educated in more conventional therapeutic disciplines such as clinical psychology, social work, and marriage and family counseling.

30 It is estimated that at least 100,000 deaths a year occur in the U.S. from alcohol related disorders, accidents, crime and suicide (U.S. Dept. of Health, 2000).

31 There are also associates of A.A., often professionals like myself, students, or relatives and friends who occasionally attend A.A. meetings, read the literature, understand some of the language and are interested in or supportive of A.A. These associates may maintain Tourist status or even become Regulars in the social world. But most often they continue their involvement only as long as they

are in a learning role, involved in research or treatment, or remain significant others of alcoholics.

[32] The first of the celebrities who received publicity surrounding their recovery was a professional baseball player named Rollie Helmsley in 1940. See AAWS 1984:236–238 and 243 n 2. An example of the kind of publicity he received can be found in the photo and story which appeared in *The Sporting News* (St. Louis, Missouri), June 27, 1940.

[33] Based on some of the data in this research which suggests that many members do not experience full integration for two or more years, it may be questionable that one year is an adequate measure of successful affiliation.

[34] Such inventories are limited in that they identify personality traits, but do not tie them to the interactional processes which may bring them about. Furthermore, they utilize terminology which is preconceived according to a psychological paradigm and can be misleading unless clearly explained. For example, in the inventories used, one term used in describing these men is "effeminate." Nevertheless, the behavioral characteristics associated with certain of these traits can be useful in defining variations in patterns of social interactions.

[35] It is estimated that as much as two years may be required for some alcoholics to fully recover neurologically (Seixas, 1982).

[36] For example, inquiring about where to sit, location of restrooms, literature prices, etc.

[37] While from a professional psychiatric perspective the A.A. practice of repeatedly introducing oneself as alcoholic has been seen as a counter-therapeutic reinforcement of the negative label (Bean, 1975), it is understood by A.A. members and pointed out by others (e.g., Grove, 1984; Smith, 1986), that the term takes on a different and positive meaning in the context of A.A. re-socialization.

[38] Perhaps invoking images of thunder and lightning bolts as in stories of God speaking to the prophets of the Old Testament.

[39] As stated in Chapter 1, these differ from the stages developed by Leach and Norris (1977) and by Rudy (1986) primarily in that they are designated by unspecified periods of time rather than specific acts or accomplishments.

[40] Rudy (1986) found 30% of his respondents were "Pure Alcoholics." That is, they believed they were alcoholic prior to coming to A.A. However, his sample was not large (100), and while I have no contrasting figures, in my own experience that percentage sounds extremely high and certainly not generalizable.

[41] This applies whether denial is defined as an unconscious defense mechanism or in a behavioral sense as a negation of the diagnosis or label of alcoholism.

[42] Coercive measures applied in social control programs such as jails and mental institutions where alcoholics have been subjected to demeaning tasks, restraints,

condemnations, threats of punishment, etc., have never been shown to be effective, possibly in part because they focus on a negative rather than a positive self-concept, or because "brainwashing," even where it appears to take, cannot be well-sustained in a relatively open society.

[43] It is interesting to note that one of the oldest approaches to skid-row alcoholism has been through the work of the Salvation Army which, from a historical perspective, has a quasi-revivalist approach. Nevertheless, this approach has not been widely effective in our heterogeneous culture where drinking is normative social behavior, so that even the Salvation Army programs now employ a combination of A.A. and professional counseling.

[44] Sick, sick person, or sickness on pages 18, 64, 67, 90, 92, 100, 101, 106, 107, 108, 115, 139, 140, 141, 147, 149, 153, 157, and 164. Ill or illness on pages 7, 18, 20, 30, 44, 92, 107, 108, 115, 118, 122, 139, 140, and 142. The words ail or ailment are used on pages 135, 139, 140. Malady appears on pages 23, 64, 92, 138, 139, and 165. (AAWS, 1976)

[45] Even in this fairly large type font, the meat of the book is contained in only 164 pages, but the term "Big Book" has continued to be used to refer to all subsequent printings and editions. The first edition came out in 1939. The third edition (AAWS 1976) was the one which was used during the period when most of the research was carried out in this study. The 164-page core of the book has remained essentially unchanged, but in 1955 (second edition), 1976 (third edition), and most recently in 2001 (fourth edition), stories at the end of the volume were added and removed for a variety of reasons, but mostly to give better representation to women, younger people, black people, and Native Americans.

[46] "Alcoholics Anonymous is a fellowship of men and women who share their experience, strength and hope with each other that they may solve their common problem and help others to recover from alcoholism."

[47] As with unruly adolescents, boundaries are clearly set, and the individual must accept responsibility for his or her own behavior.

[48] Step Twelve says "Having had a spiritual awakening as the result of these steps, we tried to carry this message to alcoholics...." referring normally to an A.A. member calling upon an alcoholic who is still drinking and not involved in the A.A. program, and inviting that person to attend A.A. meetings.

[49] "God grant me the Serenity to accept the things I cannot change, the Courage to change the things I can, and the Wisdom to know the difference." Reinhold Niebuhr taught at Union Theological Seminary in New York City from 1928–1960, and was considered in many academic circles to be one of the greatest American Protestant theologians of his generation.

[50] Even founder Bill Wilson's own mystical experiences—e.g., "I felt lifted up, as though the great clean wind of a mountain top blew through and through" (AAWS, 1976:14)—were preceded by his own intellectual explorations as well as social interactions with sober members of the Oxford Group, an A.A. precursor. (AAWS, 1976; Kurtz, 1979).

[51] Indeed, the most common theme in reports of those interviewed suggests that the actual moment of truth is most likely to occur in a moment of solitude and isolation from other humans.

[52] It can also be asserted that, despite Taylor's description (1978:107, quoted in Lofland and Skonovd, 1981:381), letdowns occur after religious revivals as well!

[53] They may not know any more about them than a first name.

[54] For a view of the impact of humor on the social construction of the A.A. self, see the study by Pollner and Stein (2001).

[55] Antabuse or disulfiram is used to prevent drinking, in that it interrupts part of the process of alcohol detoxification by the liver, and therefore makes the person sick who drinks while the medication is in the system.

About the Author

Annette Smith received her masters in social work from the University of California, Berkeley in 1961. She worked for several years as a psychiatric social worker at Napa State Hospital in California, where she helped develop an innovative co-educational unit for treating alcoholics, who had long been merely warehoused in those giant institutions. As one of the key elements in this new approach, she worked with the local A.A. Hospital and Institutions Committee in bringing A.A. to the inpatients in that program. This experience began her lifetime association with the fellowship.

After moving to San Diego in 1969, Smith worked for the County's Departments of Health and Mental Health, and in health services administration, performing clinical functions as well as developing more effective treatment services. In 1975, as County Administrator of Alcoholism services, she coordinated funding for the County's network of programs, including A.A.-based recovery homes. She helped establish the local chapter of the Employee Assistance Professional Association, taught classes at local colleges, conducted community workshops, and served on several organizational boards, including that of the local affiliate of the National Council on Alcoholism and Drug Dependence.

In the early 1990s, Smith worked for the County Schools Employee Assistance Program and had a limited private practice, primarily devoted to work with alcoholics and their family members. After receiving her Ph.D. from the University of California, San Diego in 1991, she joined the faculty of the San Diego State University School of Social Work, where she developed a course in alcoholism and drug dependence practice for graduate students, and served as Coordinator of the Center on Substance Abuse. She directed several grant projects, including the production of a training film for child welfare workers in recognizing and dealing with alcohol and drug problems among clients, and the development of one of the largest Driving Under the Influence education and counseling programs in the State. She served on the statewide DUI advisory committee and continued conducting workshops and delivering presentations on alcoholism and recovery, including presentations at several national and state conferences, to the California Association of Alcoholism And Drug Administrators and Counselors, and to the local A.A. Committee on Professional Relations.

In 2004, Smith received a life-time achievement award from the San Diego Chapter of the National Association of Social Workers and the California Society for Clinical Social Work. She is now retired and living in Florida.

References

A.A. Grapevine, June 1947. "A.A. Meeting Preamble."

AAWS. 1953. *Twelve Steps and Twelve Traditions.* New York: Alcoholics Anonymous World Services.

_____. 1976. *Alcoholics Anonymous.* 3rd ed. New York: Alcoholics Anonymous World Services. Orig. pub. 1939.

_____. 1984. *Pass It On: The Story of Bill Wilson and How the A.A. Message Reached the World.* New York: Alcoholics Anonymous World Services.

_____. 1987. *1986 A.A. Membership Survey.* New York: Alcoholics Anonymous World Services.

_____. 1990. "1989 Membership Survey Reflects Trends." *1989 A.A. Membership Survey.* New York: Alcoholics Anonymous World Services.

_____. 2001. *Alcoholics Anonymous.* 4th ed. New York: Alcoholics Anonymous World Services. Orig. pub. 1939.

_____. 2005. *2004 A.A. Membership Survey.* New York: Alcoholics Anonymous World Services.

Alexander, Jack. 1941. "Alcoholics Anonymous." *Saturday Evening Post,* March 1941, pp. 9–11.

Antonovsky, Aaron. 1980. *Health, Stress and Coping.* San Francisco: Jossey-Bass Publishing.

Bales, Robert F. 1945. "Social Therapy for a Social Disorder: Compulsive Drinking." *Journal of Social Issues* 1(3):1–9.

Bateson, Gregory. 1972. "The Cybernetics of Self: A Theory of Alcoholism." *Psychiatry* 34(February):1–18.

Bean, Margaret. 1975. "Alcoholics Anonymous." *Psychiatric Annals* 5 and 6 (February and March).

Becker, Howard. 1963. *Outsiders: Studies in the Sociology of Deviance.* New York: The Free Press.

Beckman, Linda J. 1973. "Women Alcoholics: A Review of Social and Psychological Studies." *Journal of Studies on Alcohol* 36(7):797–824.

Berger, Peter L. and Thomas Luckman. 1966. *The Social Construction of Reality: A Treatise in the Sociology of Knowledge.* Garden City, New York: Doubleday & Co.

Big Book—see AAWS (1976, 2001).

Bishop, Charles, Jr. and Bill Pittman. 1989. *The Annotated Bibliography of Alcoholics Anonymous, 1939–1989.* Wheeling, West Virginia: The Bishop of Books.

_____. 1994. *To Be Continued—The Alcoholics Anonymous World Bibliography, 1935–1994.* Wheeling, West Virginia: The Bishop of Books.

Blocker, Jack S., Jr. (ed.). 1979. *Alcohol, Reform and Society: The Liquor Issue in Social Context.* Westport, Connecticut: Greenwood Press.

Blumberg, Leonard. 1977. "The Ideology of a Therapeutic Social Movement: Alcoholics Anonymous." *Quarterly Journal of Studies on Alcohol* 38(11):122–143.

Borchert, William. 1989. "My Name is Bill W." Television movie, Daniel Petrie, director. Hallmark Hall of Fame. ABC-TV. April 30, 1989.

Bridgman, L. P. 1987. "Success of Alcoholics Anonymous: Locus of Control and God's General Revelation." *Journal of Psychobiology and Theology* 15(2):124–131.

Brown, Stephanie. 1985. *Treating the Alcoholic: A Developmental Model of Recovery.* New York: Wiley-Interscience Publication.

Brundage, V. 1985. "Gregory Bateson, Alcoholics Anonymous and Stoicism." *Psychiatry* 48(1):40–51.

Button, A. D. 1956. "Psychodynamics of Alcoholism." *Quarterly Journal of Studies in Alcoholism* 17:454–457.

Charmaz, K. C. 1980. "The Social Construction of Self-pity in the Chronically Ill." Pp. 143–146 in *Studies in Symbolic Interaction,* edited by N. K. Denzin. Greenwich, Connecticut: JAI.

Chesnut, Glenn F. 2006. *Changed by Grace: V. C. Kitchen, the Oxford Group, and A.A.* Hindsfoot Foundation Series on Spirituality and Theology. New York: iUniverse.

Conrad, Peter and Joseph W. Schneider. 1980. *Deviance and Medicalization: From Badness to Sickness.* St. Louis: C.V. Mosby.

Denzin, Norman K. 1987. *The Recovering Alcoholic.* Beverly Hills: Sage Publications.

Festinger, Leon. 1957. *A Theory of Cognitive Dissonance.* Palo Alto, California: Stanford University Press.

Gellman, Irving Peter. 1964. *The Sober Alcoholic: An Organizational Analysis of Alcoholics Anonymous.* New Haven: Yale University Press.

Gordis, Enoch. 1998. "The Neurobiology of Alcohol Abuse and Alcoholism." Pp. 9–11 in *Drug and Alcohol Dependence.* Rockville, Maryland: National Institute on Alcohol Abuse and Alcoholism (NIAAA).

Groesbeck, B. L. 1958. "Toward Description of Personality in Terms of Configuration of Motives." Pp. 383–399 in *Motives in Fantasy, Action and Society,* edited by J. W. Atkinson. Princeton: D. Van Nostrand.

Grove, Kathleen. 1984. "Becoming an Alcoholic Woman: Another Look at Labeling Theory." *California Sociologist* (Winter 1984):13–31.

Gusfield, Joseph. 1966. *Symbolic Crusade: Status Politics and the American Temperance Movement.* Urbana: University of Illinois Press.

"Hollywood & Vine." 1957. Educational film, Jon Fredricks, producer. Carpenteria, California: FMS Productions.

Howland, Richard W. A. B. and Joe W. Howland. 1978. "200 Years of Drinking in the U.S.: Evolution of the Disease Concept." Pp. 39–60 in *Drinking Alcohol in American Society,* edited by John A. Ewing and Beatrice A. Rouse. Chicago: Nelson Hall.

Jensen, George H. 2000. *Storytelling in A.A.* Carbondale: Southern Illinois University Press.

Jules-Rosette, Benetta. 1975. *American Apostles: Ritual and Conversion in the Church of John Maranke.* Ithaca, New York: Cornell University Press.

Kurtz, Ernest. 1979. *Not-God: A History of Alcoholics Anonymous.* Center City, Minn: Hazelden.

_____. 2002. "Alcoholics Anonymous and the Disease Concept of Alcoholism." *Alcoholism Treatment Quarterly* 20(Nos. 3/4):5–40.

Kurtz, Linda Farris. 1997. *Self-help and Support Groups: A Handbook for Practitioners.* Thousand Oaks, California: Sage Publications.

Leach, Barry and John L. Norris. 1977. "Factors in the Development of Alcoholics Anonymous." Pp.441–543 in *The Biology of Alcoholism: Treatment and Rehabilitation of the Chronic Alcoholic,* edited by Benjamin Kissin and Henri Begleiter. New York: Plenum Press.

Lender, Mark E. and James K. Martin. 1982. *Drinking in America: A History.* New York: The Free Press.

Lofland, John. 1960. "Initial Interaction of Newcomers in A.A.: A Field Experiment in Class Symbols and Socialization." *Social Problems 8* (Fall):102–111.

Lofland, John and Norman Skonovd. 1981. "Conversion Motifs." *Journal for the Scientific Study of Religion* 20(4):373–385.

Makela, Klaus *et al.* 1996. *A.A. as a Mutual Self-help Movement.* Madison: University of Wisconsin Press.

Maxwell, Milton A. 1984. *The A.A. Experience: A Closeup View for Professionals.* New York: McGraw-Hill.

Mead, George H. 1934. *Mind, Self and Society.* Chicago: University of Chicago Press.

Mechanic, David. 1978. *Medical Sociology.* 2nd ed. London: The Free Press.

Mills, C. Wright. 1961. *The Sociological Imagination.* New York: Grove Press.

Murphy, Mary Martha. 1952. *Social Class Differences in Responsiveness to the Program of Alcoholics Anonymous.* Doctoral dissertation, Department of Education, University of Chicago.

National Institute of Alcohol Abuse and Alcoholism, Division of Biometry and Epidemiology. 1985. "Where Do the Numbers Come From?" Pp. 5–6 in *Alcohol Use and Abuse.* Bethesda, Maryland: NIAAA No. 7PH278 (January).

O'Halloran, Sean. 2003. "Participant Observation of Alcoholics Anonymous: Contrasting Roles of the Ethnographer and Ethnomethodologist." *The Qualitative Report* 8(1):81–89.

Olson, Nancy. 2003. *With a Lot of Help from Our Friends: The Politics of Alcoholism.* Edited by Glenn F. Chesnut. Hindsfoot Foundation Series on the History of Alcoholism Treatment. New York: iUniverse, Writers Club Press.

Parsons, Talcott and Renee Fox. 1952. "Illness, Therapy and the Modern Urban American Family." *The Journal of Social Issues* 8(4):31–34.

Pollner, Melvin and Jill Stein. 2001. "Doubled Over in Laughter: Humor and the Construction of Selves in Alcoholics Anonymous." Pp. 46–63 in *Institutional Selves: Troubled Identities in a Postmodern World,* edited by Jaber F. Gubrium and James A. Holstein. New York: Oxford University Press.

Room, Robin. 1993. "Alcoholics Anonymous as a Social Movement." Pp. 167–187 in *Research on Alcoholics Anonymous: Opportunities and Alternatives,* edited by Barbara S. McCrady and William R. Miller. New Brunswick: Rutgers Center of Alcohol Studies.

Rooney, Elizabeth A. 1985. "Transformation of the Self-concept: Alcoholism and Drug Addiction Within the Medical Profession." Paper delivered at the Annual Meeting of the Pacific Sociological Association, 1985. Albuquerque, New Mexico.

Rudy, David R. 1986. *Becoming Alcoholic: Alcoholics Anonymous and the Reality of Alcoholism.* Carbondale: Southern Illinois University Press.

Sandmaier, Marian. 1980. *The Invisible Alcoholics: Women and Alcohol Abuse in America.* New York: McGraw-Hill.

Seixas, Frank A. 1982. "The Course of Alcoholism." Pp. 68–76 in *Alcoholism: Developments, Consequences and Interventions.* 2nd ed. Edited by Nada J. Estes and M. Edith Heinemann. St. Louis: C.V. Mosby.

Shibutani, Tamotsu. 1961. *Society and Personality: An Interactionist Approach to Social Psychology.* Englewood Cliffs, New Jersey: Prentice Hall.

Smith, Annette R. 1986. "Alcoholism and Gender: Patterns of Diagnosis and Response." *Journal of Drug Issues* 16(3):407–420.

_____. 1993. "The Social Construction of Group Dependency in Alcoholics Anonymous." *Journal of Drug Issues* 23(4):689–704.

The Sporting News (St. Louis, Missouri), June 27, 1940. Front page story and photo on Rollie Helmsley.

Strauss, Anselm. 1978. "A Social World Perspective." *Studies in Symbolic Interaction* 1:119–128.

Taylor, David. 1978. "The Social Organization of Recruitment in the Unification Church." Master of Arts thesis in Sociology, University of Montana.

Thune, Carl E. 1977. "Alcoholism and the Archetypal Past: A Phenomenological Perspective on Alcoholics Anonymous." *Journal of Studies on Alcohol* 38:75–88.

Tiebout, Harry M. 1944. "Conversion as a Psychological Phenomenon." Read before the New York Psychiatric Society on April 11, 1944. Available as reprint from the National Council on Alcoholism, 733 Third Avenue, New York NY 10017.

Travisano, Richard. 1970. "Alternation and Conversion as Qualitatively Different Transformations." Pp. 594–606 in *Social Psychology Through Symbolic Interaction,* edited by G. P. Stone and H. A. Farberman. Waltham, Massachusetts: Ginn-Blaisdell.

Trice, Harrison M. 1956. "A Study of the Process of Affiliation with Alcoholics Anonymous." *Quarterly Journal of Studies on Alcoholism* 18:39–54.

_____. 1957. "Sociological Factors in Association with A.A." *The Journal of Criminal Law, Criminology and Police Science* 48(4):378–386.

_____. 1958. "Alcoholics Anonymous." *The Annals of the American Academy of Political and Social Science* 315(January 1958):108–116.

Trice, H. M. and P. Roman. 1970a. "Delabeling, Relabeling and Alcoholics Anonymous." *Social Problems* 17(4):538–546.

_____. 1970b. "Sociopsychological Predictors of Affiliation with Alcoholics Anonymous." *Social Psychiatry* 5:51–59.

Trice, H. M. and W. J. Staudenmeier. 1989. "A Sociocultural History of Alcoholics Anonymous." Pp. 11–35 in *Recent Developments in Alcoholism* 3, edited by Marc Galanter. New York: Plenum Press.

Twenty-Four Hour book—see Walker (1948).

United States Department of Health and Human Services. 1987. *Sixth Special Report to the U.S. Congress on Alcohol and Health.* DHHS Publication No. (ADM) 87–1519. Washington, D.C.: U.S. Government Printing Office.

_____. 1990. *Seventh Special Report to the U.S. Congress on Alcohol and Health,* edited by Peter L. Petrakis. DHHS Publication No. (ADM) 90–1656. Washington, D.C.: U.S. Government Printing Office.

_____. 2000. *Tenth Special Report to the U.S. Congress on Alcohol and Health.* NIH Publication No. (ADM) 00–1583, Washington, D.C: U.S. Government Printing Office.

Unruh, David R. 1979. "Characteristics and Types of Participation in Social Worlds." *Symbolic Interaction* 2(2):115–129.

_____. 1980. "The Social Organization of Older People: A Social World Perspective." *Studies in Symbolic Interaction* 3:147–170.

_____. 1983. *Invisible Lives: Social Worlds of the Aged.* Beverly Hills: Sage Publications.

Vaillant, George. 1984. *The Natural History of Alcoholism.* Cambridge: Harvard University Press.

Walker, Richmond. 1948. *Twenty-Four Hours a Day.* Originally printed and distributed by the A.A. Group in Daytona Beach, Florida. Published since 1954 by Hazelden (Center City, Minnesota), the current revised edition bears a 1975 copyright.

Westerman, Robert Cecil. 1978. *The Structure of Formal and Informal Situations.* Ann Arbor: University Microfilms International.

White, William L. 1998. *Slaying the Dragon: The History of Addiction Treatment and Recovery in America.* Bloomington, Illinois: Chestnut Health Systems Publications.

Wilcox, Danny M. 1998. *Alcoholic Thinking, Language, Culture and Belief in Alcoholics Anonymous.* Westport, Connecticut: Praeger Publishers.

Wilson, Bill. 1958. "Problems Other Than Alcohol: What Can Be Done About Them." *The A.A. Grapevine,* February 1958, pp. 6–10.

York, Phyllis, David York and Ted Wachtel. 1985. *Toughlove Solutions.* Toronto: Bantam Books.

Index

978-0-595-47692-3
0-595-47692-9

www.ingramcontent.com/pod-product-compliance
Lightning Source LLC
Chambersburg PA
CBHW022253290526
45785CB00015B/753